THIS IS YOUR **PASSBOOK**® FOR ...

CASE WORKER

NLC®

NATIONAL LEARNING CORPORATION®
passbooks.com

PASSBOOK® SERIES

THE *PASSBOOK® SERIES* has been created to prepare applicants and candidates for the ultimate academic battlefield – the examination room.

At some time in our lives, each and every one of us may be required to take an examination – for validation, matriculation, admission, qualification, registration, certification, or licensure.

Based on the assumption that every applicant or candidate has met the basic formal educational standards, has taken the required number of courses, and read the necessary texts, the *PASSBOOK® SERIES* furnishes the one special preparation which may assure passing with confidence, instead of failing with insecurity. Examination questions – together with answers – are furnished as the basic vehicle for study so that the mysteries of the examination and its compounding difficulties may be eliminated or diminished by a sure method.

This book is meant to help you pass your examination provided that you qualify and are serious in your objective.

The entire field is reviewed through the huge store of content information which is succinctly presented through a provocative and challenging approach – the question-and-answer method.

A climate of success is established by furnishing the correct answers at the end of each test.

You soon learn to recognize types of questions, forms of questions, and patterns of questioning. You may even begin to anticipate expected outcomes.

You perceive that many questions are repeated or adapted so that you can gain acute insights, which may enable you to score many sure points.

You learn how to confront new questions, or types of questions, and to attack them confidently and work out the correct answers.

You note objectives and emphases, and recognize pitfalls and dangers, so that you may make positive educational adjustments.

Moreover, you are kept fully informed in relation to new concepts, methods, practices, and directions in the field.

You discover that you arre actually taking the examination all the time: you are preparing for the examination by "taking" an examination, not by reading extraneous and/or supererogatory textbooks.

In short, this PASSBOOK®, used directedly, should be an important factor in helping you to pass your test.

CASEWORKER

DUTIES

Assesses, formulates, and carries out plans to meet the needs of the individual or family; provides counseling to motivate the individual or family to increase their own capacity and confidence in their ability to handle problems; studies the background and need for care of children referred, securing information from the child himself, the family, relatives, neighbors, schools, churches, family courts and other agencies; when foster care is necessary, determines whether the child's needs can best be met in an institution or a foster family home; plans with parents and relatives for the care of children and reestablishment and stabilization of the home; establishes a relationship with individuals and families to persuade them to avail themselves of recommended social, medical, psychiatric, etc., services; identifies the need for services through in-depth discussions with clients; maintains liaison with various individual agencies to which individuals and families can be referred for services; works closely with other staff personnel, such as homemakers, in carrying out the plan for services; reviews existing case records for available information for use in formulating a plan of treatment; periodically reviews cases to determine changes in the individual's or family's situations affecting need for service.

SCOPE OF THE WRITTEN TEST

The multiple-choice written test will cover knowledge, skills, and/or abilities in such areas as:
1. Establishing and maintaining effective helping relationships in a social casework setting;
2. Interviewing; and
3. Preparing written material.

———

HOW TO TAKE A TEST

I. YOU MUST PASS AN EXAMINATION

A. *WHAT EVERY CANDIDATE SHOULD KNOW*

Examination applicants often ask us for help in preparing for the written test. What can I study in advance? What kinds of questions will be asked? How will the test be given? How will the papers be graded?

As an applicant for a civil service examination, you may be wondering about some of these things. Our purpose here is to suggest effective methods of advance study and to describe civil service examinations.

Your chances for success on this examination can be increased if you know how to prepare. Those "pre-examination jitters" can be reduced if you know what to expect. You can even experience an adventure in good citizenship if you know why civil service exams are given.

B. *WHY ARE CIVIL SERVICE EXAMINATIONS GIVEN?*

Civil service examinations are important to you in two ways. As a citizen, you want public jobs filled by employees who know how to do their work. As a job seeker, you want a fair chance to compete for that job on an equal footing with other candidates. The best-known means of accomplishing this two-fold goal is the competitive examination.

Exams are widely publicized throughout the nation. They may be administered for jobs in federal, state, city, municipal, town or village governments or agencies.

Any citizen may apply, with some limitations, such as the age or residence of applicants. Your experience and education may be reviewed to see whether you meet the requirements for the particular examination. When these requirements exist, they are reasonable and applied consistently to all applicants. Thus, a competitive examination may cause you some uneasiness now, but it is your privilege and safeguard.

C. *HOW ARE CIVIL SERVICE EXAMS DEVELOPED?*

Examinations are carefully written by trained technicians who are specialists in the field known as "psychological measurement," in consultation with recognized authorities in the field of work that the test will cover. These experts recommend the subject matter areas or skills to be tested; only those knowledges or skills important to your success on the job are included. The most reliable books and source materials available are used as references. Together, the experts and technicians judge the difficulty level of the questions.

Test technicians know how to phrase questions so that the problem is clearly stated. Their ethics do not permit "trick" or "catch" questions. Questions may have been tried out on sample groups, or subjected to statistical analysis, to determine their usefulness.

Written tests are often used in combination with performance tests, ratings of training and experience, and oral interviews. All of these measures combine to form the best-known means of finding the right person for the right job.

II. HOW TO PASS THE WRITTEN TEST

A. NATURE OF THE EXAMINATION

To prepare intelligently for civil service examinations, you should know how they differ from school examinations you have taken. In school you were assigned certain definite pages to read or subjects to cover. The examination questions were quite detailed and usually emphasized memory. Civil service exams, on the other hand, try to discover your present ability to perform the duties of a position, plus your potentiality to learn these duties. In other words, a civil service exam attempts to predict how successful you will be. Questions cover such a broad area that they cannot be as minute and detailed as school exam questions.

In the public service similar kinds of work, or positions, are grouped together in one "class." This process is known as *position-classification*. All the positions in a class are paid according to the salary range for that class. One class title covers all of these positions, and they are all tested by the same examination.

B. FOUR BASIC STEPS

1) Study the announcement

How, then, can you know what subjects to study? Our best answer is: "Learn as much as possible about the class of positions for which you've applied." The exam will test the knowledge, skills and abilities needed to do the work.

Your most valuable source of information about the position you want is the official exam announcement. This announcement lists the training and experience qualifications. Check these standards and apply only if you come reasonably close to meeting them.

The brief description of the position in the examination announcement offers some clues to the subjects which will be tested. Think about the job itself. Review the duties in your mind. Can you perform them, or are there some in which you are rusty? Fill in the blank spots in your preparation.

Many jurisdictions preview the written test in the exam announcement by including a section called "Knowledge and Abilities Required," "Scope of the Examination," or some similar heading. Here you will find out specifically what fields will be tested.

2) Review your own background

Once you learn in general what the position is all about, and what you need to know to do the work, ask yourself which subjects you already know fairly well and which need improvement. You may wonder whether to concentrate on improving your strong areas or on building some background in your fields of weakness. When the announcement has specified "some knowledge" or "considerable knowledge," or has used adjectives like "beginning principles of..." or "advanced ... methods," you can get a clue as to the number and difficulty of questions to be asked in any given field. More questions, and hence broader coverage, would be included for those subjects which are more important in the work. Now weigh your strengths and weaknesses against the job requirements and prepare accordingly.

3) Determine the level of the position

Another way to tell how intensively you should prepare is to understand the level of the job for which you are applying. Is it the entering level? In other words, is this the position in which beginners in a field of work are hired? Or is it an intermediate or advanced level? Sometimes this is indicated by such words as "Junior" or "Senior" in the class title. Other jurisdictions use Roman numerals to designate the level – Clerk I, Clerk II, for example. The word "Supervisor" sometimes appears in the title. If the level is not indicated by the title, check the description of duties. Will you be working under very close supervision, or will you have responsibility for independent decisions in this work?

4) Choose appropriate study materials

Now that you know the subjects to be examined and the relative amount of each subject to be covered, you can choose suitable study materials. For beginning level jobs, or even advanced ones, if you have a pronounced weakness in some aspect of your training, read a modern, standard textbook in that field. Be sure it is up to date and has general coverage. Such books are normally available at your library, and the librarian will be glad to help you locate one. For entry-level positions, questions of appropriate difficulty are chosen – neither highly advanced questions, nor those too simple. Such questions require careful thought but not advanced training.

If the position for which you are applying is technical or advanced, you will read more advanced, specialized material. If you are already familiar with the basic principles of your field, elementary textbooks would waste your time. Concentrate on advanced textbooks and technical periodicals. Think through the concepts and review difficult problems in your field.

These are all general sources. You can get more ideas on your own initiative, following these leads. For example, training manuals and publications of the government agency which employs workers in your field can be useful, particularly for technical and professional positions. A letter or visit to the government department involved may result in more specific study suggestions, and certainly will provide you with a more definite idea of the exact nature of the position you are seeking.

III. KINDS OF TESTS

Tests are used for purposes other than measuring knowledge and ability to perform specified duties. For some positions, it is equally important to test ability to make adjustments to new situations or to profit from training. In others, basic mental abilities not dependent on information are essential. Questions which test these things may not appear as pertinent to the duties of the position as those which test for knowledge and information. Yet they are often highly important parts of a fair examination. For very general questions, it is almost impossible to help you direct your study efforts. What we can do is to point out some of the more common of these general abilities needed in public service positions and describe some typical questions.

1) General information

Broad, general information has been found useful for predicting job success in some kinds of work. This is tested in a variety of ways, from vocabulary lists to questions about current events. Basic background in some field of work, such as sociology or economics, may be sampled in a group of questions. Often these are principles which have become familiar to most persons through exposure rather than through formal training. It is difficult to advise you how to study for these questions; being alert to the world around you is our best suggestion.

2) Verbal ability

An example of an ability needed in many positions is verbal or language ability. Verbal ability is, in brief, the ability to use and understand words. Vocabulary and grammar tests are typical measures of this ability. Reading comprehension or paragraph interpretation questions are common in many kinds of civil service tests. You are given a paragraph of written material and asked to find its central meaning.

3) Numerical ability

Number skills can be tested by the familiar arithmetic problem, by checking paired lists of numbers to see which are alike and which are different, or by interpreting charts and graphs. In the latter test, a graph may be printed in the test booklet which you are asked to use as the basis for answering questions.

4) Observation

A popular test for law-enforcement positions is the observation test. A picture is shown to you for several minutes, then taken away. Questions about the picture test your ability to observe both details and larger elements.

5) Following directions

In many positions in the public service, the employee must be able to carry out written instructions dependably and accurately. You may be given a chart with several columns, each column listing a variety of information. The questions require you to carry out directions involving the information given in the chart.

6) Skills and aptitudes

Performance tests effectively measure some manual skills and aptitudes. When the skill is one in which you are trained, such as typing or shorthand, you can practice. These tests are often very much like those given in business school or high school courses. For many of the other skills and aptitudes, however, no short-time preparation can be made. Skills and abilities natural to you or that you have developed throughout your lifetime are being tested.

Many of the general questions just described provide all the data needed to answer the questions and ask you to use your reasoning ability to find the answers. Your best preparation for these tests, as well as for tests of facts and ideas, is to be at your physical and mental best. You, no doubt, have your own methods of getting into an exam-taking mood and keeping "in shape." The next section lists some ideas on this subject.

IV. KINDS OF QUESTIONS

Only rarely is the "essay" question, which you answer in narrative form, used in civil service tests. Civil service tests are usually of the short-answer type. Full instructions for answering these questions will be given to you at the examination. But in case this is your first experience with short-answer questions and separate answer sheets, here is what you need to know:

1) Multiple-choice Questions

Most popular of the short-answer questions is the "multiple choice" or "best answer" question. It can be used, for example, to test for factual knowledge, ability to solve problems or judgment in meeting situations found at work.

A multiple-choice question is normally one of three types—

- It can begin with an incomplete statement followed by several possible endings. You are to find the one ending which *best* completes the statement, although some of the others may not be entirely wrong.
- It can also be a complete statement in the form of a question which is answered by choosing one of the statements listed.
- It can be in the form of a problem – again you select the best answer.

Here is an example of a multiple-choice question with a discussion which should give you some clues as to the method for choosing the right answer:

When an employee has a complaint about his assignment, the action which will *best* help him overcome his difficulty is to
- A. discuss his difficulty with his coworkers
- B. take the problem to the head of the organization
- C. take the problem to the person who gave him the assignment
- D. say nothing to anyone about his complaint

In answering this question, you should study each of the choices to find which is best. Consider choice "A" – Certainly an employee may discuss his complaint with fellow employees, but no change or improvement can result, and the complaint remains unresolved. Choice "B" is a poor choice since the head of the organization probably does not know what assignment you have been given, and taking your problem to him is known as "going over the head" of the supervisor. The supervisor, or person who made the assignment, is the person who can clarify it or correct any injustice. Choice "C" is, therefore, correct. To say nothing, as in choice "D," is unwise. Supervisors have and interest in knowing the problems employees are facing, and the employee is seeking a solution to his problem.

2) True/False Questions

The "true/false" or "right/wrong" form of question is sometimes used. Here a complete statement is given. Your job is to decide whether the statement is right or wrong.

SAMPLE: A roaming cell-phone call to a nearby city costs less than a non-roaming call to a distant city.

This statement is wrong, or false, since roaming calls are more expensive.
This is not a complete list of all possible question forms, although most of the others are variations of these common types. You will always get complete directions for

answering questions. Be sure you understand *how* to mark your answers – ask questions until you do.

V. RECORDING YOUR ANSWERS

Computer terminals are used more and more today for many different kinds of exams.

For an examination with very few applicants, you may be told to record your answers in the test booklet itself. Separate answer sheets are much more common. If this separate answer sheet is to be scored by machine – and this is often the case – it is highly important that you mark your answers correctly in order to get credit.

An electronic scoring machine is often used in civil service offices because of the speed with which papers can be scored. Machine-scored answer sheets must be marked with a pencil, which will be given to you. This pencil has a high graphite content which responds to the electronic scoring machine. As a matter of fact, stray dots may register as answers, so do not let your pencil rest on the answer sheet while you are pondering the correct answer. Also, if your pencil lead breaks or is otherwise defective, ask for another.

Since the answer sheet will be dropped in a slot in the scoring machine, be careful not to bend the corners or get the paper crumpled.

The answer sheet normally has five vertical columns of numbers, with 30 numbers to a column. These numbers correspond to the question numbers in your test booklet. After each number, going across the page are four or five pairs of dotted lines. These short dotted lines have small letters or numbers above them. The first two pairs may also have a "T" or "F" above the letters. This indicates that the first two pairs only are to be used if the questions are of the true-false type. If the questions are multiple choice, disregard the "T" and "F" and pay attention only to the small letters or numbers.

Answer your questions in the manner of the sample that follows:

32. The largest city in the United States is
   A. Washington, D.C.
   B. New York City
   C. Chicago
   D. Detroit
   E. San Francisco

1) Choose the answer you think is best. (New York City is the largest, so "B" is correct.)
2) Find the row of dotted lines numbered the same as the question you are answering. (Find row number 32)
3) Find the pair of dotted lines corresponding to the answer. (Find the pair of lines under the mark "B.")
4) Make a solid black mark between the dotted lines.

VI. BEFORE THE TEST

Common sense will help you find procedures to follow to get ready for an examination. Too many of us, however, overlook these sensible measures. Indeed, nervousness and fatigue have been found to be the most serious reasons why applicants fail to do their best on civil service tests. Here is a list of reminders:

- Begin your preparation early – Don't wait until the last minute to go scurrying around for books and materials or to find out what the position is all about.
- Prepare continuously – An hour a night for a week is better than an all-night cram session. This has been definitely established. What is more, a night a week for a month will return better dividends than crowding your study into a shorter period of time.
- Locate the place of the exam – You have been sent a notice telling you when and where to report for the examination. If the location is in a different town or otherwise unfamiliar to you, it would be well to inquire the best route and learn something about the building.
- Relax the night before the test – Allow your mind to rest. Do not study at all that night. Plan some mild recreation or diversion; then go to bed early and get a good night's sleep.
- Get up early enough to make a leisurely trip to the place for the test – This way unforeseen events, traffic snarls, unfamiliar buildings, etc. will not upset you.
- Dress comfortably – A written test is not a fashion show. You will be known by number and not by name, so wear something comfortable.
- Leave excess paraphernalia at home – Shopping bags and odd bundles will get in your way. You need bring only the items mentioned in the official notice you received; usually everything you need is provided. Do not bring reference books to the exam. They will only confuse those last minutes and be taken away from you when in the test room.
- Arrive somewhat ahead of time – If because of transportation schedules you must get there very early, bring a newspaper or magazine to take your mind off yourself while waiting.
- Locate the examination room – When you have found the proper room, you will be directed to the seat or part of the room where you will sit. Sometimes you are given a sheet of instructions to read while you are waiting. Do not fill out any forms until you are told to do so; just read them and be prepared.
- Relax and prepare to listen to the instructions
- If you have any physical problem that may keep you from doing your best, be sure to tell the test administrator. If you are sick or in poor health, you really cannot do your best on the exam. You can come back and take the test some other time.

VII. AT THE TEST

The day of the test is here and you have the test booklet in your hand. The temptation to get going is very strong. Caution! There is more to success than knowing the right answers. You must know how to identify your papers and understand variations in the type of short-answer question used in this particular examination. Follow these suggestions for maximum results from your efforts:

1) Cooperate with the monitor

The test administrator has a duty to create a situation in which you can be as much at ease as possible. He will give instructions, tell you when to begin, check to see that you are marking your answer sheet correctly, and so on. He is not there to guard you, although he will see that your competitors do not take unfair advantage. He wants to help you do your best.

2) Listen to all instructions

Don't jump the gun! Wait until you understand all directions. In most civil service tests you get more time than you need to answer the questions. So don't be in a hurry. Read each word of instructions until you clearly understand the meaning. Study the examples, listen to all announcements and follow directions. Ask questions if you do not understand what to do.

3) Identify your papers

Civil service exams are usually identified by number only. You will be assigned a number; you must not put your name on your test papers. Be sure to copy your number correctly. Since more than one exam may be given, copy your exact examination title.

4) Plan your time

Unless you are told that a test is a "speed" or "rate of work" test, speed itself is usually not important. Time enough to answer all the questions will be provided, but this does not mean that you have all day. An overall time limit has been set. Divide the total time (in minutes) by the number of questions to determine the approximate time you have for each question.

5) Do not linger over difficult questions

If you come across a difficult question, mark it with a paper clip (useful to have along) and come back to it when you have been through the booklet. One caution if you do this – be sure to skip a number on your answer sheet as well. Check often to be sure that you have not lost your place and that you are marking in the row numbered the same as the question you are answering.

6) Read the questions

Be sure you know what the question asks! Many capable people are unsuccessful because they failed to *read* the questions correctly.

7) Answer all questions

Unless you have been instructed that a penalty will be deducted for incorrect answers, it is better to guess than to omit a question.

8) Speed tests

It is often better NOT to guess on speed tests. It has been found that on timed tests people are tempted to spend the last few seconds before time is called in marking answers at random – without even reading them – in the hope of picking up a few extra points. To discourage this practice, the instructions may warn you that your score will be "corrected" for guessing. That is, a penalty will be applied. The incorrect answers will be deducted from the correct ones, or some other penalty formula will be used.

9) Review your answers

  If you finish before time is called, go back to the questions you guessed or omitted to give them further thought. Review other answers if you have time.

10) Return your test materials

  If you are ready to leave before others have finished or time is called, take ALL your materials to the monitor and leave quietly. Never take any test material with you. The monitor can discover whose papers are not complete, and taking a test booklet may be grounds for disqualification.

VIII. EXAMINATION TECHNIQUES

1) Read the general instructions carefully. These are usually printed on the first page of the exam booklet. As a rule, these instructions refer to the timing of the examination; the fact that you should not start work until the signal and must stop work at a signal, etc. If there are any *special* instructions, such as a choice of questions to be answered, make sure that you note this instruction carefully.

2) When you are ready to start work on the examination, that is as soon as the signal has been given, read the instructions to each question booklet, underline any key words or phrases, such as *least, best, outline, describe* and the like. In this way you will tend to answer as requested rather than discover on reviewing your paper that you *listed without describing*, that you selected the *worst* choice rather than the *best* choice, etc.

3) If the examination is of the objective or multiple-choice type – that is, each question will also give a series of possible answers: A, B, C or D, and you are called upon to select the best answer and write the letter next to that answer on your answer paper – it is advisable to start answering each question in turn. There may be anywhere from 50 to 100 such questions in the three or four hours allotted and you can see how much time would be taken if you read through all the questions before beginning to answer any. Furthermore, if you come across a question or group of questions which you know would be difficult to answer, it would undoubtedly affect your handling of all the other questions.

4) If the examination is of the essay type and contains but a few questions, it is a moot point as to whether you should read all the questions before starting to answer any one. Of course, if you are given a choice – say five out of seven and the like – then it is essential to read all the questions so you can eliminate the two that are most difficult. If, however, you are asked to answer all the questions, there may be danger in trying to answer the easiest one first because you may find that you will spend too much time on it. The best technique is to answer the first question, then proceed to the second, etc.

5) Time your answers. Before the exam begins, write down the time it started, then add the time allowed for the examination and write down the time it must be completed, then divide the time available somewhat as follows:

- If 3-1/2 hours are allowed, that would be 210 minutes. If you have 80 objective-type questions, that would be an average of 2-1/2 minutes per question. Allow yourself no more than 2 minutes per question, or a total of 160 minutes, which will permit about 50 minutes to review.
- If for the time allotment of 210 minutes there are 7 essay questions to answer, that would average about 30 minutes a question. Give yourself only 25 minutes per question so that you have about 35 minutes to review.

6) The most important instruction is to *read each question* and make sure you know what is wanted. The second most important instruction is to *time yourself properly* so that you answer every question. The third most important instruction is to *answer every question*. Guess if you have to but include something for each question. Remember that you will receive no credit for a blank and will probably receive some credit if you write something in answer to an essay question. If you guess a letter – say "B" for a multiple-choice question – you may have guessed right. If you leave a blank as an answer to a multiple-choice question, the examiners may respect your feelings but it will not add a point to your score. Some exams may penalize you for wrong answers, so in such cases *only*, you may not want to guess unless you have some basis for your answer.

7) Suggestions
   a. Objective-type questions
      1. Examine the question booklet for proper sequence of pages and questions
      2. Read all instructions carefully
      3. Skip any question which seems too difficult; return to it after all other questions have been answered
      4. Apportion your time properly; do not spend too much time on any single question or group of questions
      5. Note and underline key words – *all, most, fewest, least, best, worst, same, opposite,* etc.
      6. Pay particular attention to negatives
      7. Note unusual option, e.g., unduly long, short, complex, different or similar in content to the body of the question
      8. Observe the use of "hedging" words – *probably, may, most likely,* etc.
      9. Make sure that your answer is put next to the same number as the question
      10. Do not second-guess unless you have good reason to believe the second answer is definitely more correct
      11. Cross out original answer if you decide another answer is more accurate; do not erase until you are ready to hand your paper in
      12. Answer all questions; guess unless instructed otherwise
      13. Leave time for review

   b. Essay questions
      1. Read each question carefully
      2. Determine exactly what is wanted. Underline key words or phrases.
      3. Decide on outline or paragraph answer

4. Include many different points and elements unless asked to develop any one or two points or elements
5. Show impartiality by giving pros and cons unless directed to select one side only
6. Make and write down any assumptions you find necessary to answer the questions
7. Watch your English, grammar, punctuation and choice of words
8. Time your answers; don't crowd material

8) Answering the essay question

Most essay questions can be answered by framing the specific response around several key words or ideas. Here are a few such key words or ideas:

M's: manpower, materials, methods, money, management
P's: purpose, program, policy, plan, procedure, practice, problems, pitfalls, personnel, public relations
   a. Six basic steps in handling problems:
      1. Preliminary plan and background development
      2. Collect information, data and facts
      3. Analyze and interpret information, data and facts
      4. Analyze and develop solutions as well as make recommendations
      5. Prepare report and sell recommendations
      6. Install recommendations and follow up effectiveness

   b. Pitfalls to avoid
      1. *Taking things for granted* – A statement of the situation does not necessarily imply that each of the elements is necessarily true; for example, a complaint may be invalid and biased so that all that can be taken for granted is that a complaint has been registered
      2. *Considering only one side of a situation* – Wherever possible, indicate several alternatives and then point out the reasons you selected the best one
      3. *Failing to indicate follow up* – Whenever your answer indicates action on your part, make certain that you will take proper follow-up action to see how successful your recommendations, procedures or actions turn out to be
      4. *Taking too long in answering any single question* – Remember to time your answers properly

IX. AFTER THE TEST

Scoring procedures differ in detail among civil service jurisdictions although the general principles are the same. Whether the papers are hand-scored or graded by machine we have described, they are nearly always graded by number. That is, the person who marks the paper knows only the number – never the name – of the applicant. Not until all the papers have been graded will they be matched with names. If other tests, such as training and experience or oral interview ratings have been given, scores will be combined. Different parts of the examination usually have different weights. For example, the written test might count 60 percent of the final grade, and a rating of training and experience 40 percent. In many jurisdictions, veterans will have a certain number of points added to their grades.

After the final grade has been determined, the names are placed in grade order and an eligible list is established. There are various methods for resolving ties between those who get the same final grade – probably the most common is to place first the name of the person whose application was received first. Job offers are made from the eligible list in the order the names appear on it. You will be notified of your grade and your rank as soon as all these computations have been made. This will be done as rapidly as possible.

People who are found to meet the requirements in the announcement are called "eligibles." Their names are put on a list of eligible candidates. An eligible's chances of getting a job depend on how high he stands on this list and how fast agencies are filling jobs from the list.

When a job is to be filled from a list of eligibles, the agency asks for the names of people on the list of eligibles for that job. When the civil service commission receives this request, it sends to the agency the names of the three people highest on this list. Or, if the job to be filled has specialized requirements, the office sends the agency the names of the top three persons who meet these requirements from the general list.

The appointing officer makes a choice from among the three people whose names were sent to him. If the selected person accepts the appointment, the names of the others are put back on the list to be considered for future openings.

That is the rule in hiring from all kinds of eligible lists, whether they are for typist, carpenter, chemist, or something else. For every vacancy, the appointing officer has his choice of any one of the top three eligibles on the list. This explains why the person whose name is on top of the list sometimes does not get an appointment when some of the persons lower on the list do. If the appointing officer chooses the second or third eligible, the No. 1 eligible does not get a job at once, but stays on the list until he is appointed or the list is terminated.

X. HOW TO PASS THE INTERVIEW TEST

The examination for which you applied requires an oral interview test. You have already taken the written test and you are now being called for the interview test – the final part of the formal examination.

You may think that it is not possible to prepare for an interview test and that there are no procedures to follow during an interview. Our purpose is to point out some things you can do in advance that will help you and some good rules to follow and pitfalls to avoid while you are being interviewed.

What is an interview supposed to test?

The written examination is designed to test the technical knowledge and competence of the candidate; the oral is designed to evaluate intangible qualities, not readily measured otherwise, and to establish a list showing the relative fitness of each candidate – as measured against his competitors – for the position sought. Scoring is not on the basis of "right" and "wrong," but on a sliding scale of values ranging from "not passable" to "outstanding." As a matter of fact, it is possible to achieve a relatively low score without a single "incorrect" answer because of evident weakness in the qualities being measured.

Occasionally, an examination may consist entirely of an oral test – either an individual or a group oral. In such cases, information is sought concerning the technical knowledges and abilities of the candidate, since there has been no written examination for this purpose. More commonly, however, an oral test is used to supplement a written examination.

Who conducts interviews?

The composition of oral boards varies among different jurisdictions. In nearly all, a representative of the personnel department serves as chairman. One of the members of the board may be a representative of the department in which the candidate would work. In some cases, "outside experts" are used, and, frequently, a businessman or some other representative of the general public is asked to serve. Labor and management or other special groups may be represented. The aim is to secure the services of experts in the appropriate field.

However the board is composed, it is a good idea (and not at all improper or unethical) to ascertain in advance of the interview who the members are and what groups they represent. When you are introduced to them, you will have some idea of their backgrounds and interests, and at least you will not stutter and stammer over their names.

What should be done before the interview?

While knowledge about the board members is useful and takes some of the surprise element out of the interview, there is other preparation which is more substantive. It *is* possible to prepare for an oral interview – in several ways:

1) Keep a copy of your application and review it carefully before the interview

This may be the only document before the oral board, and the starting point of the interview. Know what education and experience you have listed there, and the sequence and dates of all of it. Sometimes the board will ask you to review the highlights of your experience for them; you should not have to hem and haw doing it.

2) Study the class specification and the examination announcement

Usually, the oral board has one or both of these to guide them. The qualities, characteristics or knowledges required by the position sought are stated in these documents. They offer valuable clues as to the nature of the oral interview. For example, if the job involves supervisory responsibilities, the announcement will usually indicate that knowledge of modern supervisory methods and the qualifications of the candidate as a supervisor will be tested. If so, you can expect such questions, frequently in the form of a hypothetical situation which you are expected to solve. NEVER go into an oral without knowledge of the duties and responsibilities of the job you seek.

3) Think through each qualification required

Try to visualize the kind of questions you would ask if you were a board member. How well could you answer them? Try especially to appraise your own knowledge and background in each area, *measured against the job sought*, and identify any areas in which you are weak. Be critical and realistic – do not flatter yourself.

4) Do some general reading in areas in which you feel you may be weak

For example, if the job involves supervision and your past experience has NOT, some general reading in supervisory methods and practices, particularly in the field of human relations, might be useful. Do NOT study agency procedures or detailed manuals. The oral board will be testing your understanding and capacity, not your memory.

5) Get a good night's sleep and watch your general health and mental attitude

You will want a clear head at the interview. Take care of a cold or any other minor ailment, and of course, no hangovers.

What should be done on the day of the interview?

Now comes the day of the interview itself. Give yourself plenty of time to get there. Plan to arrive somewhat ahead of the scheduled time, particularly if your appointment is in the fore part of the day. If a previous candidate fails to appear, the board might be ready for you a bit early. By early afternoon an oral board is almost invariably behind schedule if there are many candidates, and you may have to wait. Take along a book or magazine to read, or your application to review, but leave any extraneous material in the waiting room when you go in for your interview. In any event, relax and compose yourself.

The matter of dress is important. The board is forming impressions about you – from your experience, your manners, your attitude, and your appearance. Give your personal appearance careful attention. Dress your best, but not your flashiest. Choose conservative, appropriate clothing, and be sure it is immaculate. This is a business interview, and your appearance should indicate that you regard it as such. Besides, being well groomed and properly dressed will help boost your confidence.

Sooner or later, someone will call your name and escort you into the interview room. *This is it.* From here on you are on your own. It is too late for any more preparation. But remember, you asked for this opportunity to prove your fitness, and you are here because your request was granted.

What happens when you go in?

The usual sequence of events will be as follows: The clerk (who is often the board stenographer) will introduce you to the chairman of the oral board, who will introduce you to the other members of the board. Acknowledge the introductions before you sit down. Do not be surprised if you find a microphone facing you or a stenotypist sitting by. Oral interviews are usually recorded in the event of an appeal or other review.

Usually the chairman of the board will open the interview by reviewing the highlights of your education and work experience from your application – primarily for the benefit of the other members of the board, as well as to get the material into the record. Do not interrupt or comment unless there is an error or significant misinterpretation; if that is the case, do not hesitate. But do not quibble about insignificant matters. Also, he will usually ask you some question about your education, experience or your present job – partly to get you to start talking and to establish the interviewing "rapport." He may start the actual questioning, or turn it over to one of the other members. Frequently, each member undertakes the questioning on a particular area, one in which he is perhaps most competent, so you can expect each member to participate in the examination. Because time is limited, you may also expect some rather abrupt switches in the direction the questioning takes, so do not be upset by it. Normally, a board member will not pursue a single line of questioning unless he discovers a particular strength or weakness.

After each member has participated, the chairman will usually ask whether any member has any further questions, then will ask you if you have anything you wish to add. Unless you are expecting this question, it may floor you. Worse, it may start you off on an extended, extemporaneous speech. The board is not usually seeking more information. The question is principally to offer you a last opportunity to present further qualifications or to indicate that you have nothing to add. So, if you feel that a significant qualification or characteristic has been overlooked, it is proper to point it out in a sentence or so. Do not compliment the board on the thoroughness of their examination – they have been sketchy, and you know it. If you wish, merely say, "No thank you, I have nothing further to add." This is a point where you can "talk yourself out" of a good impression or fail to present an important bit of information. Remember, *you close the interview yourself.*

The chairman will then say, "That is all, Mr. _____, thank you." Do not be startled; the interview is over, and quicker than you think. Thank him, gather your belongings and take your leave. Save your sigh of relief for the other side of the door.

How to put your best foot forward

Throughout this entire process, you may feel that the board individually and collectively is trying to pierce your defenses, seek out your hidden weaknesses and embarrass and confuse you. Actually, this is not true. They are obliged to make an appraisal of your qualifications for the job you are seeking, and they want to see you in your best light. Remember, they must interview all candidates and a non-cooperative candidate may become a failure in spite of their best efforts to bring out his qualifications. Here are 15 suggestions that will help you:

1) Be natural – Keep your attitude confident, not cocky

If you are not confident that you can do the job, do not expect the board to be. Do not apologize for your weaknesses, try to bring out your strong points. The board is interested in a positive, not negative, presentation. Cockiness will antagonize any board member and make him wonder if you are covering up a weakness by a false show of strength.

2) Get comfortable, but don't lounge or sprawl

Sit erectly but not stiffly. A careless posture may lead the board to conclude that you are careless in other things, or at least that you are not impressed by the importance of the occasion. Either conclusion is natural, even if incorrect. Do not fuss with your clothing, a pencil or an ashtray. Your hands may occasionally be useful to emphasize a point; do not let them become a point of distraction.

3) Do not wisecrack or make small talk

This is a serious situation, and your attitude should show that you consider it as such. Further, the time of the board is limited – they do not want to waste it, and neither should you.

4) Do not exaggerate your experience or abilities

In the first place, from information in the application or other interviews and sources, the board may know more about you than you think. Secondly, you probably will not get away with it. An experienced board is rather adept at spotting such a situation, so do not take the chance.

5) If you know a board member, do not make a point of it, yet do not hide it

Certainly you are not fooling him, and probably not the other members of the board. Do not try to take advantage of your acquaintanceship – it will probably do you little good.

6) Do not dominate the interview

Let the board do that. They will give you the clues – do not assume that you have to do all the talking. Realize that the board has a number of questions to ask you, and do not try to take up all the interview time by showing off your extensive knowledge of the answer to the first one.

7) Be attentive

You only have 20 minutes or so, and you should keep your attention at its sharpest throughout. When a member is addressing a problem or question to you, give him your undivided attention. Address your reply principally to him, but do not exclude the other board members.

8) Do not interrupt

A board member may be stating a problem for you to analyze. He will ask you a question when the time comes. Let him state the problem, and wait for the question.

9) Make sure you understand the question

Do not try to answer until you are sure what the question is. If it is not clear, restate it in your own words or ask the board member to clarify it for you. However, do not haggle about minor elements.

10) Reply promptly but not hastily

A common entry on oral board rating sheets is "candidate responded readily," or "candidate hesitated in replies." Respond as promptly and quickly as you can, but do not jump to a hasty, ill-considered answer.

11) Do not be peremptory in your answers

A brief answer is proper – but do not fire your answer back. That is a losing game from your point of view. The board member can probably ask questions much faster than you can answer them.

12) Do not try to create the answer you think the board member wants

He is interested in what kind of mind you have and how it works – not in playing games. Furthermore, he can usually spot this practice and will actually grade you down on it.

13) Do not switch sides in your reply merely to agree with a board member

Frequently, a member will take a contrary position merely to draw you out and to see if you are willing and able to defend your point of view. Do not start a debate, yet do not surrender a good position. If a position is worth taking, it is worth defending.

14) Do not be afraid to admit an error in judgment if you are shown to be wrong

 The board knows that you are forced to reply without any opportunity for careful consideration. Your answer may be demonstrably wrong. If so, admit it and get on with the interview.

15) Do not dwell at length on your present job

 The opening question may relate to your present assignment. Answer the question but do not go into an extended discussion. You are being examined for a *new* job, not your present one. As a matter of fact, try to phrase ALL your answers in terms of the job for which you are being examined.

Basis of Rating

 Probably you will forget most of these "do's" and "don'ts" when you walk into the oral interview room. Even remembering them all will not ensure you a passing grade. Perhaps you did not have the qualifications in the first place. But remembering them will help you to put your best foot forward, without treading on the toes of the board members.

 Rumor and popular opinion to the contrary notwithstanding, an oral board wants you to make the best appearance possible. They know you are under pressure – but they also want to see how you respond to it as a guide to what your reaction would be under the pressures of the job you seek. They will be influenced by the degree of poise you display, the personal traits you show and the manner in which you respond.

ABOUT THIS BOOK

 This book contains tests divided into Examination Sections. Go through each test, answering every question in the margin. At the end of each test look at the answer key and check your answers. On the ones you got wrong, look at the right answer choice and learn. Do not fill in the answers first. Do not memorize the questions and answers, but understand the answer and principles involved. On your test, the questions will likely be different from the samples. Questions are changed and new ones added. If you understand these past questions you should have success with any changes that arise. Tests may consist of several types of questions. We have additional books on each subject should more study be advisable or necessary for you. Finally, the more you study, the better prepared you will be. This book is intended to be the last thing you study before you walk into the examination room. Prior study of relevant texts is also recommended. NLC publishes some of these in our Fundamental Series. Knowledge and good sense are important factors in passing your exam. Good luck also helps. So now study this Passbook, absorb the material contained within and take that knowledge into the examination. Then do your best to pass that exam.

———

EXAMINATION SECTION

EXAMINATION SECTION
TEST 1

DIRECTIONS: Each question or incomplete statement is followed by several suggested answers or completions. Select the one that BEST answers the question or completes the statement. *PRINT THE LETTER OF THE CORRECT ANSWER IN THE SPACE AT THE RIGHT.*

1. The primary function of the Department of Social Services is to

1._____

   A. refer needy persons to legally responsible relatives for support
   B. enable needy persons to become self-supporting
   C. refer ineligible persons to private agencies
   D. grant aid to needy eligible persons
   E. administer public assistance programs in which the federal and state governments do not participate

2. A public assistance program objective should be designed to

2._____

   A. provide for eligible persons in accordance with their individual requirements and with consideration of the circumstances in which they live
   B. provide for eligible persons at a standard of living equal to that enjoyed while they were self-supporting
   C. make sure that assistance payments from public funds are not too liberal
   D. guard against providing a better living for persons receiving aid than is enjoyed by the most frugal independent families
   E. eliminate the need for private welfare agencies

3. It is often stated that it would be better to abolish the need for relief rather than to extend the existing public assistance programs.
This statement suggests that

3._____

   A. existing legislation makes it too east for people to apply for and receive assistance
   B. public assistance should be limited to institutional care for rehabilitative purposes
   C. the support of needy persons should be the responsibility of their own families and relatives rather than that of the government
   D. the existing criteria used to determine *need* for public assistance are too liberal and should be modified to include a *work test*
   E. attempts should be made to eradicate those forces in our social organization which cause poverty

4. The one of the following types of public assistance which is frequently described as a *special privilege* is

4._____

   A. veteran assistance
   B. emergency assistance
   C. aid to dependent children
   D. old-age assistance
   E. vocational rehabilitation of the handicapped

5. The principle of *settlement* holds that each community is responsible for the care of its own members and that communities should not bear the costs of care for needy non-residents.
   This was an intrinsic principle of the

   A. English Poor Laws
   B. Home Rule Amendment
   C. Single Tax Proposal
   D. National Bankruptcy Regulations
   E. Proportional Representation Act

6. The FIRST form of state social security legislation developed in the United States was

   A. health insurance
   B. unemployment compensation
   C. workmen's compensation
   D. old-age insurance
   E. old-age assistance

7. The plan for establishing a federal department with Cabinet status to be known as the Department of Health, Education, and Welfare, was

   A. vetoed by the President after having been passed by Congress
   B. disapproved by the Senate after having been passed by the House of Representatives
   C. rejected by both the Senate and the House of Representatives
   D. enacted into legislation during a past session of Congress
   E. determined to be unconstitutional

8. Census Bureau reports show certain definite social trends in our population. One of these trends which was a major contributing factor in the establishment of the federal old-age insurance system was the

   A. increased rate of immigration to the United States
   B. rate at which the number of Americans living to 65 years of age and beyond is increasing
   C. increasing amounts spent for categorical relief in the country as a whole
   D. decreasing number of legally responsible relatives who have been unable to assist the aged since the depression of 1929
   E. number of states which have failed to meet their obligations in the care of the aged

9. The Federal Housing Administration is the agency which

   A. insures mortgages made by lending institutions for new construction or remodeling of old construction
   B. provides federal aid for state and local governments for slum clearance and housing for very low income families
   C. subsidizes the building industry through direct grants
   D. provides for the construction of low-cost housing projects owned and operated by the federal government
   E. combines city planning with government subsidies for large-scale housing

5._____

6._____

7._____

8._____

9._____

10. Reports show that more men than women are physically handicapped MAINLY because

    10._____

    A. women are instinctively more cautious than men
    B. men are more likely to have congenital deformities
    C. women tend to seek surgical remedies because of greater concern over personal appearance
    D. men have lower ability to recover from injury
    E. men are more likely to be exposed to hazardous conditions

11. Of the following, the explanation married women give MOST frequently for seeking employment outside the home is that they wish to

    11._____

    A. escape the drudgeries of home life
    B. develop secondary employment skills
    C. maintain an emotionally satisfying career
    D. provide the main support for the family
    E. supplement the family income

12. Of the following home conditions, the one MOST LIKELY to cause emotional disturbances in children is

    12._____

    A. increased birthrate following the war
    B. disrupted family relationships
    C. lower family income than that of neighbors
    D. higher family income than that of neighbors
    E. overcrowded living conditions

13. Casual unemployment, as distinguished from other types of unemployment, is traceable MOST readily to

    13._____

    A. a decrease in the demand for labor as a result of scientific progress
    B. more of less haphazard changes in the demand for labor in certain industries
    C. periodic changes in the demand for labor in certain industries
    D. disturbances and disruptions in industry resulting from international trade barriers
    E. increased mobility of the population

14. Labor legislation, although primarily intended for the benefit of the employee, may aid the employer by

    14._____

    A. increasing his control over the immediate labor market
    B. prohibiting government interference with operating policies
    C. protecting him, through equalization of labor costs, from being under-cut by other employers
    D. transferring to the general taxpayer the principal costs of industrial hazards of accident and unemployment
    E. increasing the pensions of civil service employees

15. When employment and unemployment figures both decline, the MOST   15._____
probable conclusion is that

    A. the population has reached a condition of equilibrium
    B. seasonal employment has ended
    C. the labor force has decreased
    D. payments for unemployment insurance have been increased
    E. industrial progress has reduced working hours

16. In evaluating the adequacy of an individual's income, a social service   16._____
worker should place primary emphasis on

    A. its value in relation to the average income
    B. the source of the income
    C. its relation to the earning capacity of the individual
    D. its purchasing power
    E. the purposes for which it is spent

17. An individual with an I.Q. of 100 may be said to have demonstrated   17._____
_____ intelligence.

    A. superior   B. absolute
    C. substandard   D. approximately average
    E. high average

18. While state legislatures differ in many respects, all of them are MOST   18._____
NEARLY alike in

    A. provisions for retirement of members
    B. rate of pay
    C. length of legislative sessions
    D. method of selection of their members
    E. length of term of office

19. If a state passed a law in a field under Congressional jurisdiction and if Con-   19._____
gress subsequently passed contrary legislation, the state provision would
be

    A. regarded as never having existed
    B. valid until the next session of the state legislature which would be
        obliged to repeal it
    C. superseded by the federal statute
    D. ratified by Congress
    E. still operative in the state involved

20. Power to pardon offenses committed against the people of the United States is vested in the

    A. Supreme Court of the United States
    B. United States District Courts
    C. Federal Bureau of Investigation
    D. United States Parole Board
    E. President of the United States

20._____

21. As distinguished from formal social control of an individual's behavior, an example of informal social control is that exerted by

    A. public opinion
    B. religious doctrine
    C. educational institutions
    D. statutes
    E. public health measures

21._____

22. The PRINCIPAL function of the jury in a jury trial is to decide questions of

    A. equity
    B. fact
    C. injunction
    D. contract
    E. law

22._____

23. Of the following rights of an individual, the one which usually depends on citizenship as distinguished from those given anyone living under the laws of the United States is the right to

    A. receive public assistance
    B. hold an elective office
    C. petition the government for redress of grievances
    D. receive equal protection of the laws
    E. be accorded a trial by jury

23._____

24. The name of Thomas Malthus is MOST CLOSELY associated with a work on

    A. population
    B. political justice
    C. capitalism
    D. social contract
    E. wealth of nations

24._____

25. A chronic functional disease characterized by fits or attacks in which there is a loss of consciousness with a succession of convulsions is called

    A. epilepsy
    B. dipsomania
    C. catalepsy
    D. Hodgkin's disease
    E. paresis

25._____

KEY (CORRECT ANSWERS)

1. D	11. E	21. A
2. A	12. B	22. B
3. E	13. B	23. B
4. A	14. C	24. A
5. A	15. C	25. A
6. C	16. D	
7. D	17. D	
8. B	18. D	
9. A	19. C	
10. E	20. E	

TEST 2

Questions 1-10.

DIRECTIONS: Questions 1 to 10 inclusive are based on the following table, which gives a partial summary of certain groups of cases in the social services center of a public assistance agency.

SOCIAL SERVICES CENTER CASELOAD SUMMARY, June-September

	June	July	August	September
Total Cases Under Care at				
End of Month	13, 790	11, 445	13,191	12, 209
Home relief	4, 739	2, 512	6, 055	5, 118
Old-age assistance	5, 337	b	5, 440	2, 265
Aid to dependent children	3, 487	1, 621	1, 520	4, 594
Aid to the blind	227	251	176	232
Net Change during Month	- 344	c	1, 746	- 982
Applications Made during Month	1, 542	789	3,153	1, 791
Total Cases Accepted during				
Month	534	534	2,879	982
Home relief	278	213	342	338
Old-age assistance	43	161	1, 409	f
Aid to dependent children	195	153	1,115	307
Aid to the blind	18	7	13	14
Total cases Closed during				
Month	878	d	1, 133	1, 964
To private employment	326	1, 197	460	870
To unemployment insurance	96	421	126	205
Reclassified	176	326	178	399
All other reasons	280	935	e	490
Total Cases Carried Over to Next Month	a	11, 445	13,191	12, 209

1. The number which should be placed in the blank indicated by *a* is   1._____

    A. 12,912   B. 13,446
    C. 13,790   D. 14,134
    E. none of the foregoing

2. The number which should be placed in the blank indicated by *b* is 2._____

    A. 6,385   B. 7,601
    C. 8,933   D. 7,061
    E. none of the foregoing

3. The number which should be placed in the blank indicated by *c* is 3._____

    A. -2,345   B. -344
    C. 344   D. 3,413
    E. none of the foregoing

4. The number which should be placed in the blank indicated by *d* is 4._____

    A. 2,789   B. 2,345
    C. 7,601   D. 3,879
    E. none of the foregoing

5. Of the total number of cases closed during the month of August, the percentage closed for reasons other than reclassification or receipt of unemployment insurance is APPROXIMATELY 5._____

    A. 13.8%   B. 73.17%   C. 26.83%   D. 40.60%   E. 24.63%

6. In comparing June and July, the figures indicate that with respect to the total cases under care at the end of each month, 6._____

    A. the percentage of total cases accepted during the month was lower in June
    B. the percentage of total cases accepted during the month was higher in June
    C. the percentage of total cases accepted during both months was the same
    D. there were more cases under care at the end of July
    E. there is insufficient data for comparison of the total cases under care at the end of each month

7. The total number of cases accepted during the entire period in the category in which most cases were accepted was 7._____

    A. 1,409   B. 1,936   C. 1,770   D. 4,929   E. 20,103

8. In comparing July and September, the figures indicate that 8._____

    A. more cases were closed in September because of private employment
    B. the total number of cases accepted during the month consisted of a greater proportion of home relief cases in September
    C. in one of these months, there were more total cases under care at the end of the month than at the beginning of the month
    D. aid to dependent children cases at the beginning of September numbered almost three times as many as at the beginning of July
    E. none of the foregoing is correct

8

9. The total number of applications made during the four-month period was   9._____

   A. more than four times the number of cases closed because of private employment during the same period
   B. less than the combined totals of aid-to-dependent children cases under care in June and July
   C. 4,376 more than the total number of cases accepted during August
   D. 23 times as large as the number of cases reclassified in July
   E. 5,916 less than the total number of cases carried over to September

10. The ratio of old-age assistance cases accepted in August to the total number of such cases under care at the end of that month is expressed with the GREATEST degree of accuracy by the figures   10._____

   A. 1:4   B. 1:25   C. 4:1   D. 7:128   E. 10:39

11. The term *mores* refers to   11._____

   A. English meadows   B. bribery
   C. Moorish worship   D. telegraphic code
   E. social customs

12. *Disparity* refers MOST directly to   12._____

   A. difference   B. argument
   C. low wages   D. separation
   E. injustice

13. The technical term used to express the ratio between mental and chronological age is called the   13._____

   A. mentality rating   B. culture level index
   C. psychometric standard   D. achievement index
   E. intelligence quotient

14. In social services work, the disorganizing factors in a personal or familial situation which prevent or hinder rehabilitation are called   14._____

   A. median deviations   B. transference situations
   C. rank correlations   D. liabilities
   E. collective representations

15. The period in the life of man when mental abilities begin to deteriorate is known as   15._____

   A. puberty   B. adolescence
   C. gerontology   D. senility
   E. antiquity

Questions 16 - 25.

DIRECTIONS: Questions 16 to 25 inclusive contain two blank spaces each. You are to select
the words which will fill the blanks so that the sentence will be true and sensible. For the *first* blank in each question, select a word or phrase preceded by
letter A,B,C,D, or E. For the *second* blank in the question, select a word or
phrase preceded by letter V,W,X,Y, or Z. Use the two letters you have selected
as your answer and print both these letters in the correspondingly numbered
space on the Answer Sheet.

16. _____ is to public assistance as citizenship is to _____.   16._____

    A. need   B. school attendance
    C. worthiness   D. child
    E. welfare center
    V. passport   W. alien
    X. immigration   Y. excise tax
    Z. indictment

17. _____is to home relief as public institutional care is to _____.   17._____

    A. compensation   B. supplementation
    C. direct relief   D. survivor's insurance
    E. fiscal period
    V. removal of custody   W. adoption
    X. indoor relief   Y. day care
    Z. voucher assistance

18. _____ is to *face sheet* as income is to _____.   18._____

    A. client   B. cash relief
    C. relief standard   D. case record
    E. emergency assistance
    V. wages   W. home
    X. debts   Y. taxes
    Z. bonus

19. _____ is to demography as man is to _____.   19._____

    A. politics   B. racial relations
    C. stigmata   D. social statistics
    E. democracy
    V. population   W. geography
    X. woman   Y. marriage
    Z. anthropology

20. _____ is to tuberculosis as Terman is to _____.   20._____

    A. Wassermann   B. Mantoux
    C. Schick   D. Ascheim-Zondek
    E. Snellen
    V. litmus test   W. means test
    X. lie detector test   Y. intelligence test
    Z. CAVD test

21. _____ is to dementia as feeblemindedness is to_____.   21._____

    A. anger   B. luxation
    C. insanity   D. diagnosis
    E. psychiatry
    V. myopia   W. amentia
    X. tibia   Y. criminal
    Z. childhood

22. Frustration is to _____ as _____ is to relaxation.   22._____

    A. satisfaction   B. goal
    C. need   D. desire
    E. motive
    V. tension   W. behavior
    X. adjustment   Y. readjustment
    Z. reaction

23. _____ is to embezzlement as parole is to _____.   23._____

    A. intent   B. larceny
    C. desertion   D. guilt
    E. conviction
    V. bail   W. plea
    X. probation   Y. innocence
    Z. reformatory

24. Abandonment is to _____ as coercion is to _____.   24._____

    A. abduction   B. discovery
    C. guardian   D. adultery
    E. desertion
    V. desertion   W. impotence
    X. crime   Y. coition
    Z. constraint

25. _____ is to homicide as felony is to _____.   25._____

    A. courthouse   B. mayhem
    C. negligence   D. witness
    E. manslaughter
    V. judge   W. crime
    X. autopsy   Y. civil suit
    Z. prosecutor

11

KEY (CORRECT ANSWERS)

1. C	11. E	21. CW
2. D	12. A	22. AV
3. A	13. E	23. BX
4. E	14. D	24. EZ
5. B	15. D	25. EW
6. A	16. AV	
7. B	17. CX	
8. E	18. DV	
9. E	19. DZ	
10. E	20. BY	

TEST 3

Questions 1-3.

DIRECTIONS: Questions 1 to 3 inclusive are based on the following passage:

Aid to dependent children shall be given to a parent or other relative as herein specified for the benefit of a child or children under sixteen years of age or of a minor or minors between sixteen and eighteen years of age if in the judgment of the administrative agency: (1) the granting of an allowance will be in the interest of such child or minor, and (2) the parent or other relative is a fit person to bring up such child or minor so that his physical, mental, and moral well-being will be safeguarded, and (3) aid is necessary to enable such parent or other relative to do so, and (4) such child or minor is a resident of the state on the date of application for aid, and (5) such minor between sixteen and eighteen years of age is regularly attending school in accordance with the regulations of the department. An allowance may be granted for the aid of such child or minor who has been deprived or parental support or care by reason of the death, continued absence from the home, or physical or mental incapacity of a parent, and who is living with his father, mother, grandfather, grandmother, brother, sister, stepfather, stepmother, stepbrother, stepsister, uncle or aunt. In making such allowances, consideration shall be given to the ability of the relative making application and of any other relatives to support and care for or to contribute to the support and care of such child or minor. In making all such allowances, it shall be made certain that the religious faith of the child or minor shall be preserved and protected.

1. The preceding passage is concerned primarily with

   1._____

   A. the financial ability of persons applying for public assistance
   B. compliance on the part of applicants with the *settlement* provisions of the law
   C. the fitness of parents or other relatives to bring up physically, mentally, or morally delinquent children between the ages of sixteen and eighteen
   D. eligibility for aid to dependent children
   E. the religious faith of children or minors coming within the provisions of this law

2. On the basis of the preceding passage, the MOST accurate of the following statements is:

   2._____

   A. Mary Doe, mother of John, age 18, is entitled to aid for her son if he is attending school regularly.
   B. Evelyn Stowe, mother of Eleanor, age 13, is not entitled to aid for Eleanor if she uses her home for immoral purposes.
   C. Ann Roe, cousin of Helen, age 14, is entitled to aid for Helen if the latter is living with her.
   D. Peter Moe, uncle of Henry, age 15, is not entitled to aid for Henry if the latter is living with him.
   E. Harriet Hoe, mother of Paul, age 7, is not entitled to aid for him if she has been divorced from her husband.

3. The passage quoted above is PROBABLY an excerpt of the

   3._____

   A. Administrative Code   B. Social Welfare Law
   C. Federal Security Act   D. City Charter
   E. Colonial Laws of the state

4. Recent amendment of the Social Security Act has produced major changes in the administration of public assistance. The one of the following which is NOT included among these changes is the   4._____

    A. availability of federal funds in matching payments for home relief to veterans who are employable but unemployed
    B. establishment of federal grants-in-aid for a category of assistance to be known as aid to the permanently and totally disabled
    C. extension of the four categories of assistance to Puerto Rico and the Virgin Islands
    D. sharing by the federal government of costs of assistance to needy aged and blind persons in public medical institutions
    E. availability of federal funds within present federal maxima in matching indirect payments for medical care in old-age assistance, aid to the blind, and aid to dependent children

5. The length of residence required to make a person eligible for the various forms of public assistance available in the United States   5._____

    A. is the same in all states but is different among public assistance programs in a given state
    B. is the same in all states and among different public assistance programs in a given state
    C. is the same in all states for different categories
    D. varies among states and among different public assistance programs in a given state
    E. varies only in the local agencies of a given state

6. The Social Welfare Law requires that whenever an applicant for aid to dependent children resides in a place where there is a central index or a social service exchange, the public welfare official shall register the case with such index or exchange.   6._____
    This requirement is for the purpose of

    A. preventing duplication and coordinating the work of public and private agencies
    B. establishing prior claims on the amounts of assistance furnished when repayments are made
    C. having the social service exchange determine which agency should handle the case
    D. providing statistical data regarding the number of persons receiving grants for aid to dependent children
    E. making sure that opportunities for private employment are available to persons receiving assistance

7. A person who knowingly brings a needy person from another state into the State for the purpose of making him a public charge, is guilty of   7._____

    A. violation of the Displaced Persons Act
    B. violation of the Mann Act
    C. a felony
    D. a misdemeanor
    E. no offense

8. Among the following needy persons, the one NOT eligible to receive vet-   8._____
eran assistance is the

    A. husband of a veteran, if living with the veteran
    B. minor grandchild of a veteran, if living with the veteran
    C. incapacitated child of a deceased veteran
    D. stepmother or stepfather of a veteran, if living with the veteran
    E. non-veteran brother or sister of a veteran, if living with the veteran

9. The term *state residence,* as defined in the Social Welfare Law, means con-   9._____
tinuous residence within the state for a period of at least

    A. one year   B. two years
    C. six months   D. one month
    E. one day

10. In order to be eligible for old-age assistance in this State, applicants must   10._____
have resided continuously in the state prior to the date of application for

    A. three months   B. six months
    C. one year   D. five years
    E. no specific period

11. Under the Social Security Act, public assistance payments do NOT provide   11._____
for

    A. old-age assistance   B. care of children in foster homes
    C. aid to the blind   D. aid to dependent children
    E. aid to the permanently and totally disabled

12. The Social Welfare Law provides that certain relatives of a recipient of pub-   12._____
lic assistance or care, or of a person liable to become in need thereof, be
responsible for the support of such person if they are of sufficient ability.
The one of the following who is NOT a legally responsible relative is a(n)

    A. mother   B. child
    C. grandparent   D. uncle
    E. step-parent, for a minor stepchild

13. Of the following, the distinguishing characteristics of a *dependent child* as   13._____
defined in the Social Welfare Law, refer to a child who is

    A. in the custody of, or wholly or partly maintained by an authorized orga-
nization of charitable, eleemosynary, correctional, or reformatory
character
    B. in such condition of want or suffering or who is under such improper
guardianship as to injure or endanger the morals of himself or others
    C. between 16 and 18 years of age and solely dependent upon his par-
ents for support and maintenance
    D. under 16 years of age and deserted or abandoned by parents or other
persons lawfully charged with his care
    E. incorrigible or ungovernable and beyond the control of his parents or
guardian

14. Recent adoption laws tend to place increased emphasis upon   14._____

    A. informal signing of adoption papers
    B. lowered residence requirements for adoption
    C. establishment of the child's inheritance rights
    D. social investigation of the home before adoption
    E. increased boarding rates paid to adoptive parents

15. Any person or organization soliciting donations in public places is required   15._____
    to have a license issued by the

    A. Police Department
    B. Department of Sanitation
    C. Division of Labor Relations
    D. Department of Social Services
    E. Department of Licenses

16. A person who, though himself, in good health, harbors disease germs which   16._____
    may be passed on to others, is called a(n)

    A. instigator   B. carrier
    C. incubator   D. inoculator
    E. malingerer

17. Diseases most commonly caused by certain working environments or con-   17._____
    ditions are known as _____ diseases.

    A. infectious   B. contagious
    C. occupational   D. hereditary
    E. compensatory

18. The process of destroying micro-organisms which cause disease or infec-   18._____
    tion is called

    A. contamination   B. immunization
    C. inoculation   D. sterilization
    E. infestation

19. Proper utilization of the term *carious* would involve reference to   19._____

    A. teeth
    B. curiosity
    C. shipment of food packages to needy persons in Europe
    D. hazardous or precarious situations
    E. lack of reasonable precautions

20. The chemical agent which has been used extensively to prevent the spread   20._____
    of typhus infection is

    A. cortisone   B. D.D.T.
    C. penicillin   D. ephedrine
    E. sulfanilamide

21. The medical term for *hardening of the arteries* is

21._____

    A. carcinoma   B. arthritis
    C. thrombosis   D. arteriosclerosis
    E. phlebitis

22. A set of symptoms which occur together is called a

22._____

    A. sympathin   B. syncope
    C. syndrome   D. synecdoche
    E. syllogism

23. If the characteristics of a person were being studied by competent observers, it would be expected that their observations would differ MOST markedly with respect to their evaluation of the person's

23._____

    A. intelligence
    B. nutritional condition
    C. temperamental characteristics
    D. weight
    E. height

24. If there are evidences of dietary deficiency in families where cereals make up a major portion of the diet, the MOST LIKELY reason for this deficiency is that

24._____

    A. cereals cause absorption of excessive quantities of water
    B. persons who concentrate their diet on cereals do not chew their food properly
    C. carbohydrates are deleterious
    D. other essential food elements are omitted
    E. children eat cereals too rapidly

25. Although malnutrition is generally associated with poverty, dietary studies of population groups in the United States reveal that

25._____

    A. malnutrition is most often due to a deficiency of nutrients found chiefly in high-cost foods
    B. there has been overemphasis of the causal relationship between poverty and malnutrition
    C. malnutrition is found among people with sufficient money to be well fed
    D. a majority of the population in all income groups is undernourished
    E. malnutrition is not a factor in the incidence of rickets

KEY (CORRECT ANSWERS)

1. D	11. B	21. D
2. B	12. D	22. C
3. B	13. A	23. C
4. A	14. D	24. D
5. D	15. D	25. C
6. A	16. B	
7. D	17. C	
8. E	18. D	
9. A	19. A	
10. E	20. B	

TEST 4

DIRECTIONS: Each question or incomplete statement is followed by several suggested answers or completions. Select the one that BEST answers the question or completes the statement. *PRINT THE LETTER OF THE CORRECT ANSWER IN THE SPACE AT THE RIGHT.*

1. A medically trained person who treats mental diseases is called a(n)   1._____

    A. psychologist   B. sociologist
    C. psychiatrist   D. physiologist
    E. opthamologist

2. Of the following social agencies, the one which MUST rely MOST on short-   2._____
contact interviewing is the

    A. child-guidance clinic   B. Travelers' Aid Society
    C. Social Service Exchange   D. Hospital for Crippled Children
    E. juvenile court

3. The organization which has as one of its primary functions the mitigation of   3._____
suffering caused by famine, fire, floods, and other national calamities is the

    A. National Safety Council
    B. Salvation Army
    C. Public Administration Services
    D. American National Red Cross
    E. American Legion

4. The MAIN difference between public welfare and private social agencies is   4._____
that in public agencies

    A. case records are open to the public
    B. the granting of assistance cannot be sufficiently flexible to meet the
       varying needs of individual recipients
    C. only financial assistance may be provided
    D. all policies and procedures must be based upon statutory authoriza-
       tions
    E. economical and efficient administration are stressed because their
       funds are obtained through public taxation

5. Proper handling of a case in which the applicant requires temporary congre-   5._____
gate care would involve a referral initially to

    A. a private agency
    B. a religious institution
    C. the state welfare agency
    D. the federal government
    E. one of the municipal shelters

6. A recipient of relief who is in need of the services of an attorney but is unable to pay the customary fees, should generally be referred to the

    6._____

    A. Small Claims Court
    B. Domestic Relations Court
    C. County Lawyers Association
    D. City Law Department
    E. Legal Aid Society

7. A person who is not satisfied with the action taken by the Department of Social Services on his application for old-age assistance may appeal to the State Department of Social Welfare for an impartial review and a *fair hearing.*
The final decision in such a hearing is made by the

    7._____

    A. State Board of Social Welfare
    B. State Commissioner of Social Welfare
    C. Commissioner of Social Services
    D. Attorney-General of the State
    E. Federal Security Agency

8. An injured workman should file his claim for workmen's compensation with the

    8._____

    A. State Labor Relations Board
    B. Division of Placement and Unemployment Insurance
    C. State Industrial Commission
    D. Workmen's Compensation Board
    E. State Insurance Board

9. In order to supplement the care and guidance furnished to young people by the family and other social institutions, the legislature created a temporary agency known as the State Youth Commission. Among the powers and duties of this Commission are those listed below, with the EXCEPTION of

    9._____

    A. supervising the administration of state institutions for juvenile delinquents
    B. authorizing payment of state aid to municipalities in accordance with the provisions of the Youth Commission Act
    C. making studies and recommendations regarding the guidance and treatment of juvenile delinquents
    D. devising plans for the creation and operation of youth bureaus and recreation projects
    E. making necessary studies and analyses of the problems of youth guidance and the prevention of juvenile delinquency

10. One of the institutions operated by the State Department of Social Welfare is the

    10._____

    A. State School for the Blind, Batavia
    B. State Training School for Boys, Warwick
    C. State Reconstruction Home, West Haverstraw
    D. State School for Mental Defectives, Newark
    E. Woodbourne Institute for Defective Delinquents, Woodbourne

11. The one of the following which is NOT included among the responsibilities of the Bureau of Public Assistance of the Social Security Administration is 11._____

    A. reviewing and approving state plans for public assistance and the operation of these plans, in order to determine their continuing conformity to the Social Security Act

    B. administering provisions for grants by the federal government to states for old-age assistance, aid to the blind, aid to dependent children, and aid to the permanently and totally disabled

    C. carrying out the Social Security Administration's functions in connection with the federal-state unemployment insurance system

    D. reviewing state estimates for public assistance and certifying the amount of federal grants to states

    E. collecting, analyzing, and publishing data on the operation of all forms of public assistance in the states, including general assistance

12. Because of the number of able-bodied employable persons on relief, the Department of Social Services once adopted the policy of 12._____

    A. removing all employables from the relief rolls

    B. subjecting such persons to special review in order to determine whether they are concealing facts about employment

    C. assigning such persons to various city departments for appropriate employment commensurate with the amount of relief grants

    D. forcing all men on the employable list to apply to other governmental agencies as provisional civil service workers

    E. requesting selective service boards to give preference to such employable persons of appropriate age for induction into the armed forces

13. The type of insurance found MOST frequently among families such as those assisted by the Department of Social Services is 13._____

    A. accident   B. straight life
    C. endowment   D. industrial
    E. personal liability

14. Of the following items in the standard budget of the Department of Social Services, the one for which actual expenditures would be MOST constant throughout the year is 14._____

    A. fuel   B. housing
    C. medical care   D. clothing
    E. household replacements

15. The MOST frequent cause of *broken homes* is attributed to the 15._____

    A. temperamental incompatibilities of parents and in-laws

    B. extension of the system of children's courts

    C. psychopathic irresponsibility of the parents

    D. institutionalization of one of the spouses

    E. death of one or both spouses

16. In rearing children, the problems of the widower are usually greater than   16._____
those of the widow, largely because of the

    A. tendency of widowers to impose excessively rigid moral standards
    B. increased economic hardship
    C. added difficulty of maintaining a desirable home
    D. possibility that a stepmother will be added to the household
    E. prevalent masculine prejudice against pursuits which are inherently
feminine

17. Foster-home placement of children is often advocated in preference to insti-   17._____
tutionalization PRIMARILY because

    A. the law does not provide for local supervision of children's institutions
    B. institutions furnish a more expensive type of care
    C. the number of institutions is insufficient compared to the number of
children needing care
    D. children are not well treated in institutions
    E. foster homes provide a more normal environment for children

18. Of the following, the category MOST likely to yield the greatest reduction in   18._____
cost to the taxpayer under improved employment conditions is

    A. home relief, including aid to the homeless
    B. aid to the blind
    C. aid to dependent children
    D. old-age assistance
    E. aid to the permanently and totally disabled

19. One of the MOST common characteristics of the chronic alcoholic is   19._____

    A. low intelligence level   B. wanderlust
    C. psychosis   D. independence
    E. egocentricity

20. Of the following factors leading toward the cure of the alcoholic, the MOST   20._____
important is thought to be

    A. removal of all alcohol from the immediate environment
    B. development of a sense of personal adequacy
    C. social disapproval of drinking
    D. segregation from former companions
    E. intensive supervision by parole officers

21. An interview is BEST conducted in private primarily because   21._____

    A. the person interviewed will tend to be less self-conscious
    B. the interviewer will be able to maintain his continuity of thought better
    C. it will insure that the interview is *off the record*
    D. people tend to *show off* before an audience
    E. constant interruption by visitors and telephone calls will irritate the
interviewer

22. An interviewer will be better able to understand the person interviewed and his problems if he recognizes that much of the person's behavior is due to motives

    A.   which are deliberate   B.   of which he is unaware
    C.   which are inexplicable   D.   which are kept under control
    E.   which are calculated to deceive

23. When an applicant for public assistance is repeatedly told that *everything will be all right,* the effect that can usually be expected is that he will

    A.   develop overt negativistic reactions toward the agency
    B.   become too closely identified with the interviewer
    C.   doubt the interviewer's ability to understand and help with his problems
    D.   have greater confidence in the interviewer
    E.   make no appreciable change in his attitude toward the interviewer

24. While interviewing a client, it is preferable that the social service worker

    A.   take no notes in order to avoid disturbing the client
    B.   focus primary attention on the client while the client is talking
    C.   take no notes in order to impress upon the client the worker's ability to remember all the pertinent facts of his case
    D.   record all the details in order to show the client that what he says is important
    E.   record all the details in order to impress upon the client the official character of his statements

25. During an interview, a curious applicant asks several questions about the social service worker's private life. As the interviewer, you should

    A.   refuse to answer such questions
    B.   answer his questions fully
    C.   explain that your primary concern is with his problems and that discussion of your personal affairs will not be helpful in meeting his needs
    D.   explain that it is the responsibility of the interviewer to ask questions and not to answer them
    E.   answer only enough of his questions to the extent necessary to establish a friendly relationship with him

KEY (CORRECT ANSWERS)

1. C	11. C	21. A
2. B	12. C	22. B
3. D	13. D	23. C
4. D	14. B	24. C
5. E	15. E	25. C
6. E	16. C	
7. B	17. E	
8. D	18. A	
9. A	19. E	
10. B	20. B	

TEST 5

DIRECTIONS: Each question or incomplete statement is followed by several suggested answers or completions. Select the one that BEST answers the question or completes the statement. *PRINT THE LETTER OF THE CORRECT ANSWER IN THE SPACE AT THE RIGHT.*

1. An interviewer can BEST establish a good relationship with the person being interviewed by   1._____

    A. assuming casual interest in the statements made by the person being interviewed
    B. asking questions which enable the person to show pride in his knowledge
    C. taking the point of view of the person interviewed
    D. controlling the interview to a major extent
    E. showing a genuine interest in the person

2. An interviewer's attention must be directed toward himself as well as toward the person interviewed.   2._____
This statement means that the interviewer should

    A. keep in mind the extent to which his own prejudices may influence his judgment
    B. rationalize the statements made by the person interviewed
    C. gain the respect and confidence of the person interviewed
    D. avoid being too impersonal
    E. avoid using indirect methods in eliciting information from the person interviewed

3. More complete expression will be obtained from a person being interviewed if the interviewer can create the impression that   3._____

    A. the data secured will become part of a permanent record
    B. official information must be accurate in every detail
    C. it is the duty of the person interviewed to give accurate data
    D. the interviewer checks additional sources to get complete data
    E. the person interviewed is participating in a discussion of his own problems

4. The practice of asking leading questions should be avoided in an interview because the   4._____

    A. interviewer risks revealing his attitudes to the person being interviewed
    B. interviewer may be led to ignore the objective attitudes of the person interviewed
    C. answers may be unwarrantedly influenced
    D. person interviewed will resent the attempt to lead him and will be less cooperative
    E. replies to such questions are always verbose

5. A good technique for the interviewer to use in an effort to secure reliable data and to reduce the possibility of misunderstanding is to

    5._____

    A. use casual undirected conversation, enabling the person being interviewed to talk about himself, and thus secure the desired information
    B. adopt the procedure of using direct questions regularly
    C. extract the desired information from the person being interviewed by putting him on the defensive
    D. explain to the person being interviewed the information desired and the reason for needing it
    E. explain that he is an experienced interviewer and can detect false statements

6. As a social service worker interviewing an applicant for public assistance, your attitude toward his veracity should be that the information he has furnished you is

    6._____

    A. *untruthful* until you have had an opportunity to check the information
    B. *truthful* only insofar as verifiable facts are concerned
    C. *untruthful* because clients tend to interpret everything in their own favor
    D. *truthful* until you have information to the contrary
    E. *untruthful* because most applicants for public assistance are unreliable

7. When a public assistance agency assigns its most experienced interviewers to conduct initial interviews with applicants, the MOST important reason for its action is that

    7._____

    A. experienced workers are always older, and therefore command the respect of applicants
    B. the applicant may be given a complete understanding of the procedures to be followed and the time involved in obtaining assistance payments
    C. applicants with fraudulent intentions will be detected, and prevented from obtaining further services from the agency
    D. the agency may immediately obtain an accurate and complete plan to be followed in giving assistance to the applicant
    E. the applicant may be given an understanding of the purpose of the assistance program and of the bases for granting assistance, in addition to the routine information

8. As a social service worker conducting the first interview with an applicant for public assistance, you should

    8._____

    A. ask questions requiring *yes* or *no* answers in order to simplify the interview
    B. rephrase several of the key questions as a check on his previous statements
    C. let him tell his own story while keeping him to the relevant facts
    D. avoid showing any sympathy for the applicant while he is revealing his personal needs and problems
    E. ask only direct questions so as to demonstrate your impersonal approach

9. An aged person who is unable to produce immediate proof of age has made
an application for old-age assistance. He states that it will take about a
week to obtain the necessary proof and that he does not have enough
money to provide meals for himself until then.
If it appears that he is in immediate need, he should be told that

    A. the law requires proof of age before any assistance can be granted
    B. temporary assistance will be provided pending the completion of the
investigation
    C. a personal loan will be provided from a revolving fund
    D. he should arrange for a small loan from private sources
    E. he will have to produce an affidavit witnessed by two relatives who will
vouch for the accuracy of his statements before any assistance can be
provided

9._____

10. If the social service worker learns during an interview that the client has
applied for public assistance without the knowledge of her husband, even
though he is a member of the same household, the worker should

    A. appear not to notice this oversight, but watch for other evidences of
marital discord
    B. make no mention of this to the applicant, but before taking final action
send a note to the husband asking him to come in
    C. discuss this situation with the client and help her recognize the value
of her husband's participation in the application
    D. point out to the applicant the implications of her behavior and ask for
an explanation of her motives
    E. tell the applicant that the husband's needs will be excluded from the
budget until he appears for a personal interview

10._____

11. Responsibility for fully informing the public about the availability of public
assistance can MOST successfully be discharged by

    A. local public assistance agencies
    B. social service exchanges
    C. community chest organizations
    D. councils of social agencies
    E. service clubs

11._____

12. Of the sources through which a welfare agency can seek information about
the family background and economic needs of a particular client, the MOST
important consists of

    A. records and documents covering the client
    B. interviews with the client's relatives
    C. the client's own story
    D. direct contacts with former employers
    E. information offered by the client's neighbors

12._____

13. The one of the following sources of evidence which would be MOST likely to give information needed to verify residence, is

    A. family affidavits
    B. medical and hospital bills
    C. an original birth certificate
    D. rental receipts
    E. an insurance policy

13._____

14. In public assistance agencies, vital statistics are a resource used by the workers MAINLY to

    A. help establish eligibility through verification of births, deaths, and mar-
riages
    B. help establish eligibility through verification of divorce proceedings
    C. secure proof of unemployment and eligibility for unemployment com-
pensation
    D. secure indices of the cost of living in the larger cities
    E. discourage applications from ineligible persons

14._____

15. Case records should be considered confidential in order to

    A. make it impossible for agencies to know each other's methods
    B. permit worker to make objective rather than subjective comments
    C. prevent recipients from comparing amounts of assistance given to dif-
ferent families
    D. keep pertinent information from other social workers
    E. protect clients and their families

15._____

16. Because the social service worker generally is not trained as a psychiatrist, he should, when encountering psychiatric problems in the performance of his departmental duties,

    A. ignore such problems because they are beyond the scope of his
responsibilities
    B. inform the affected persons that he recognizes their problems person-
ally but will take no official cognizance of them
    C. ask to be relieved of the cases in which these problems are met and
recommend that they be assigned to a psychiatrist
    D. recognize such problems where they exist and make referrals to the
proper sources for treatment
    E. ask his supervisor to assign a psychiatric case worker to accompany
him on all subsequent visits to the client

16._____

17. The family budget is a device used by the Department of Social Services to

    A. determine changes in the cost-of-living index
    B. estimate the needs of families and the amount of assistance neces-
sary to meet these needs
    C. evaluate its financial condition
    D. estimate probable expenditures during a given period
    E. determine whether an applicant is eligible for categorical assistance
or for general relief

17._____

18. The amount included for food for each client in Department of Social Services budgets should

    18._____

    A. be based on quantitative caloric estimates of energy requirements rather than on variety in the kinds of food
    B. be high enough to provide minimum subsistence, but low enough to discourage ineligible applicants
    C. exclude special dietary needs which are relatively expensive
    D. cover food idiosyncrasies of various members of the household
    E. meet the generally accepted standards for proper nutrition

19. The program for aid to dependent children is PRIMARILY directed toward

    19._____

    A. the placement and supervision of children in selected foster homes
    B. provision of assistance whereby children can remain in their own homes or in the homes of relatives
    C. rehabilitation of neglected and delinquent children
    D. provision of specialized services to children in areas of special need
    E. provision of assistance to widows of good moral character for the care of their children

20. Since need is a condition of eligibility in the old-age assistance program, an assistance payment to an aged recipient should be based upon a consideration of

    20._____

    A. the length of time he received general relief prior to his application for old-age assistance
    B. his attitude toward the agency
    C. his total needs and resources
    D. the probable duration of his dependency
    E. the average monthly cost of institutional care

21. From a social point of view, the reason for the growth of the practice of giving public assistance in the form *of* cash payments is the

    21._____

    A. resultant reduction in complaints coming to the agency
    B. increased necessity for developing nationwide comparative statistics
    C. facilitation of recovery for relief improperly granted
    D. public's increasing belief in the essential justice of this type of assistance
    E. development of a better understanding of pressure groups

22. In closing the case of a client, the social service worker should attempt to give the client a(n)

    22._____

    A. feeling of being rejected by the agency as a worthy person
    B. idea of the progress of similar cases being handled by the agency
    C. understanding that his case could be reopened for full relief, if necessary, but not for emergency assistance
    D. explanation of the conditions upon which he might make re-application
    E. explanation of the limitations of the agency in meeting his needs

23. There is widespread agreement among nearly all planning groups concerned with public assistance that

    23._____

    A.   need for public assistance should be the primary, if not the only, condition of eligibility; and that all arbitrary conditions of eligibility such as citizenship, ownership of home, and moral character should be eliminated from all public assistance programs
    B.   public assistance grants should be paid by voucher rather than in cash because most recipients do not use cash allowances for the purposes for which they are intended
    C.   the names of persons receiving public assistance should be publicized in order to prevent fraud
    D.   public assistance should be discontinued immediately whenever the unemployed father of a family receiving assistance refuses a job offer
    E.   public assistance should not be provided for any persons who own property or who have any financial resources

24. Of fundamental importance to the work of a social worker in the Department of Social Services is

    24._____

    A.   the knowledge of when to use the power of the Department to subdue an angry client
    B.   an ability to classify clients according to common characteristics as described in case records
    C.   the ability to explain eligibility in terms of legal requirements with clarity and simplicity
    D.   the realization that persons who apply for public assistance have become dependent because of lack of industriousness and are therefore unable to manage their own affairs
    E.   a general knowledge of the executive, administrative, and supervisory functions of the Department

25. Although a social worker in the Department of Social Services has several responsibilities, his primary one is to

    25._____

    A.   nullify any restrictive rules and regulations issued by the State Department of Social Welfare
    B.   carry out his own interpretation of the function of the Department of Social Services
    C.   carry out the objectives of Department of Social Services programs as set forth in the Social Welfare Law
    D.   avoid community criticism of the manner in which the programs of the Department of Social Services are conducted
    E.   give relief to all applicants who claim they are eligible

KEY (CORRECT ANSWERS)

1. E	11. A	21. D
2. A	12. C	22. D
3. E	13. D	23. A
4. C	14. A	24. C
5. D	15. E	25. C
6. D	16. D	
7. E	17. B	
8. C	18. E	
9. B	19. B	
10. C	20. C	

EXAMINATION SECTION
TEST 1

DIRECTIONS: Each question or incomplete statement is followed by several suggested answers or completions. Select the one that BEST answers the question or completes the statement. *PRINT THE LETTER OF THE CORRECT ANSWER IN THE SPACE AT THE RIGHT.*

1. Local responsibility for the relief of economic need long having been recognized as inadequate, the state and federal governments have established schemes of *categorical* assistance and social insurance. In the preceding sentence the italicized word means MOST NEARLY

   A. conditional   B. economic   C. pecuniary   D. classified

   1.____

2. When a person *vicariously* lives out his own problems in novels and plays, he is engaging in an experience that is, in terms of the italicized word in this sentence.

   A. dynamic   B. monastic   C. substituted   D. dignified

   2.____

3. The Alcoholics Anonymous program, which in essence amounts to a *therapeutic* procedure, is codified into twelve steps.
   The italicized word in the preceding sentence means MOST NEARLY

   A. compensatory   B. curative   C. sequential   D. volitional

   3.____

4. The case of Mary Smith who ordered her husband out of the house and begged his pardon before he could leave, if accepted as characteristic behavior on the part of this woman, is BEST considered as an illustration of

   A. ambivalence   B. compensation   C. retrogression   D. frustration

   4.____

5. To say that the Community Chest movement seems to have been *indigenous* to the North American continent describes this movement, in terms of the italicized word in this sentence, MOST NEARLY as

   A. imported   B. essential
   C. native   D. homogeneous

   5.____

6. There should be no *opprobrium* attached to the term 'second-hand housing' since every house is second-hand after the first occupancy. The italicized word in the preceding sentence means MOST NEARLY

   A. stigma   B. honor   C. rank   D. credit

   6.____

7. Clinics are now seeing many people who complain of seriously disturbed feelings and other symptoms relating to *traumatic war* experiences.
   In the preceding sentence the italicized word means MOST NEARLY

   A. recent   B. worldwide   C. prodigious   D. shocking

   7.____

8. The nature of the *pathology* underlying the compulsion is obscure.
   In the preceding sentence, the italicized word means MOST NEARLY

   A. drive   B. disease
   C. deterioration   D. development

   8.____

33

9. If the interests of a social welfare agency are concerned with bringing opportunities for self-help to underprivileged *ethnic* groups, its activities involve MOST NEARLY, in terms of the italicized word in this sentence,

    A. racial factors   B. minority units
    C. religious affiliations   D. economic conditions

9.____

10. Increased facilities for medical care (though interrupted o some extent by the *exigencies* of wartime) will safeguard the health of many children who in previous generations would have been doomed to an early death or to physical disability.
In the foregoing sentence the MOST NEARLY CORRECT equivalent of the italicized word is

    A. obstacles   B. occurrences   C. extenuations   D. exactions

10.____

11. The name of Sanford Bates would be associated by a well-read social service worker with the book entitled

    A. THE FAMILY   B. SOCIAL CHANGE
    C. PRISONS AND BEYOND   D. HULL HOUSE

11.____

Questions 12-16

DIRECTIONS: In questions 12 to 16 below, Column I consists of items referring to certain characteristics of areas usually found to exist in most American cities. Column II describes four sections into which the general sociological pattern of the modern city may be divided. Select the description in Column II to which the reference in Column I is MOST appropriate.

COLUMN I	COLUMN II	
12. The area in which a predominantly male resident population would probably be found.	A. Retail stores, eating establishments, motion picture theaters, offices of professional people and business organizations	12.____
13. The area in which a *slum* would probably be located if it existed in this city.	A. Made-over private dwellings, rooming houses, cheap hotels, pawnbrokers, wholesale business establishments	13.____
14. The area in which the most prominent citizens of the community would probably be found living.	C. Less crowding than in above area, more modern houses, fewer children, wives not generally gainfully employed.	14.____
15. The area likely to contain the sparsest resident population.	D. Fashionable suburbs, homes of professional and business leaders, relative cleanliness and modernity.	15.____
16. The area likely to be inhabited by middle-class families.		16.____

17. To the social service worker who has maintained an interest in the field of psychiatry, THE NEUROTIC PERSONALITY OF OUR TIME would suggest

    A. Margaret Mead   B. R.S. Lynd and H.M. Lynd
    C. Karen Horney   D. Ruth Benedict

17.____

18. The conscientious social service worker is interested in the provisions of the Wagner-Ellender-Taft bill because the subject of this Congressional legislation is

    A. rent control   B. housing
    C. tax reduction   D. health insurance

18.____

19. Of the following, the name MOST closely identified with developments leading to the enactment of the Social Security Act was

    A. Harry Hopkins   B. William Beveridge
    C. Herbert C. Hoover   D. Arthur J. Altmeyer

19.____

20. The federal government will grant reimbursement under the Social Security Act to states for certain categories of assistance, provided the state law is in conformance with the requirements of the Act. One of the following requirements which is enforced by the federal government is that

    A. citizenship must be required as a condition of eligibility
    B. some residence requirement must be included
    C. payment to the client must be *money payment*
    D. some exemptions from merit system operation must be provided

20.____

21. Of the following social services administered by public agencies, the one administered by the federal government is

    A. unemployment compensation
    B. old age and survivors insurance
    C. vocational rehabilitation for civilians
    D. civilian war assistance

21.____

22. Most old age assistance programs have been limited in general to the financial and physical needs of the aged because

    A. it is impossible to determine their other needs with any degree of practicality
    B. social agencies are unwilling to enlarge their responsibilities for the care of the aged
    C. old people are not interested in social participation
    D. public relief administrators have not been given the means to undertake more augmented programs

22.____

23. Of the qualifications and procedures connected with the method under which an insured individual may receive old age and survivors insurance, three are given below. The statement which is NOT among these qualifications or procedures is that the individual

    A. must have been employed in covered employment for certain specified periods of time
    B. must have attained the age of 65

23.____

C. has his primary benefit amounts computed in relation to his record of earnings in covered employment
D. is disqualified to receive old age and survivors insurance benefits for any month in which he had an earned income of $100 or less

24. One of the requirements regarding an institution in which the Department of Social Service may place a neglected child is that the institution must   24.____

    A. have been certified by the State Board of Social Welfare
    B. be operated on a non-sectarian basis
    C. have been incorporated for a period of not less than three years
    D. be situated within the geographical limits of the city

25. With respect to destitute children placed out in institutions as public charges, the Commissioner of Social Services   25.____

    A. may not deputize subordinates to make an investigation of such an institution except through the Department of Licenses
    B. may reimburse such an institution for any expense, other than salaries, actually incurred in the placing out
    C. may not authorize an institution to which a child has been committed to place such a child in a family
    D. may transfer a child from one institution to another, except when either institution is governed by persons professing the same religious faith as the parents of the child

26. George Bailey, who has been unable to earn a living because of a recent Industrial accident, is referred to his nearest social services center and subsequently placed in an institution for rehabilitation and training so that he will become a permanent charge upon the public. Bailey has a son whom the social service reports as unwilling, though sufficiently able, to support his incapacitated father. If the Commissioner of Social Services wishes to compel Bailey's son to pay a reasonable charge for Bailey's care in the institution, he would apply for the necessary order to the   26.____

    A. Family Court   B. Supreme Court
    C. State Board of Social Services   D. Court of Appeals

27. Commitment by the Department of Social Services invariably implies that the parents   27.____

    A. have maltreated the child
    B. are unable to support the child
    C. have, through voluntary agreement, given custody of the child to the Commissioner of Social Services
    D. have given the child up for adoption

28. The service of the Department of Social Services which is financed jointly by the city, state, and federal governments is   28.____

    A. veterans assistance
    B. aid to dependent children
    C. home relief
    D. the cost of board in foster home care for children

29. The LEAST applicable of the following statements regarding unemployment compensation for workers in this State is

    A. the employer pays the total tax for unemployment compensation
    B. the maximum period of benefit payments is 26 weeks in any benefit year
    C. benefit payments are the same whether a person has been discharged from his job on account of retrenchment or is unemployed on account of illness
    D. employees of philanthropic and religious organizations are not included in coverage

29.____

30. Ten months ago, Mr. Johnson came to this city from Plattsburgh, New York, where he had lived for ten years. Unable to find work, he applies at your welfare center for assistance for himself and his family.
As an acting intake interviewer, you should tell Mr. Johnson that

    A. he is ineligible for relief since his needs are the responsibility of another municipality
    B. he is ineligible for relief and should return to Plattsburgh because no jobs are available in this city
    C. he should wait two more months in order to attain the required year's settlement
    D. his application is acceptable and his eligibility on the basis of need will be determined

30.____

KEY (CORRECT ANSWERS)

1. D	11. C	21. B
2. C	12. B	22. D
3. B	13. B	23. D
4. A	14. D	24. A
5. C	15. A	25. B
6. A	16. C	26. A
7. D	17. C	27. C
8. B	18. B	28. B
9. A	19. A	29. C
10. D	20. C	30. D

TEST 2

DIRECTIONS: Each question or incomplete statement is followed by several suggested answers or completions. Select the one that BEST answers the question or completes the statement. *PRINT THE LETTER OF THE CORRECT ANSWER IN THE SPACE AT THE RIGHT.*

1. A war veteran in need of public assistance and care who applies for such relief in this city will be eligible to receive such help if he   1._____

    A. had been discharged from military service only under honorable conditions
    B. is a resident of this city on the date of application for public assistance
    C. has been a state resident for a period of one year or more
    D. was a resident of the city at the time he entered the military service

2. Mrs. Doe was receiving aid to dependent children for the third year when, in the course of reinvestigation, the social service worker discovered that she had a part-time job and arranged to reduce her relief accordingly. Mrs. Doe objected to the reduction and, after discussing her case with the proper officials in the Department of Social Services, decided to file a final appeal from their decision.
A social service worker aware of the proper procedure to be followed in this case would have advised Mrs. Doe that the highest authority to which she could appeal is the   2._____

    A. Social Security Administration
    B. State Charities Aid
    C. Commissioner of Social Services
    D. State Department of Social Welfare

3. A social service worker receives complaints from neighbors that the three children of a certain relief family are being neglected by their parents to the point where their health and safety are endangered, and suggestions are made that the youngsters be separated from their negligent parents. Authority to order removal of the children from their home, if investigation substantiates these charges, is vested PRIMARILY in   3._____

    A. the Commissioner of Social Services
    B. the Society for the Prevention of Cruelty to Children
    C. a Family Court judge
    D. a police officer

4. Anthony, aged 8, has had many difficult experiences in his life. His father's whereabouts are unknown as he deserted when Anthony was two years old. His mother, whom he loved dearly, died three months ago. Since that time he has been living with his grandmother, who is old and ill, and cannot care for such an active little boy. Together the grandmother and you, the social service worker, have decided that placement in a foster home is essential for Anthony's well-being. You know he will resist any change in his living arrangements.
According to acceptable case work practice, the BEST of the following methods for you to apply in this situation is to   4._____

    A. take the boy to his new home without telling him anything beforehand
    B. explain that it is necessary to move him and that he is going to a very nice place where he will be happy and have many things he does not have now

C. tell him you are sorry if he feels bad about it, but grown-ups know best what is good for him and he will have to do what they say
D. give the child a chance to get to know you before he is moved and to express his feelings in relation to the plan which is being made for him

5. Mrs. Mary Wooster, who has been caring for her 10-year-old orphaned niece, applies for aid to dependent children when her husband's income is reduced. If you are the social service worker assigned to this case, you should tell Mrs. Wooster that her application   5.____

    A. cannot be accepted for investigation because her niece must be removed from her home and placed out by the state
    B. can be accepted for investigation because she falls within the group of relatives who are eligible to receive aid to dependent children
    C. cannot be accepted for investigation because relatives other than parents are never granted help through aid to dependent children
    D. can be accepted for investigation because her niece is her legal responsibility

6. A 15-year-old girl calls on you, the social service worker, to say that her mother is negligent and buys clothing for herself and treats her male friends to motion picture dates with her grant from aid to dependent children.
According to the MOST generally accepted social case work principles, you should tell the girl that   6.____

    A. the grant will be stopped immediately
    B. she does not have to put up with that kind of environment and can arrange to leave her mother immediately
    C. you will take this matter up with her mother and see her again at some future time
    D. she should file a formal complaint against her mother

7. Assume that in making your first visit to the home of an applicant for aid to dependent children, you find the beds unmade, the dishes unwashed, and the furniture so dusty that you cannot find a clean place to sit down, although it is already 3:00 in the afternoon. The applicant has four small children.
Under the circumstances described, you should inform the applicant that   7.____

    A. she is ineligible for the grant because she does not give her children the proper physical environment
    B. her application will be investigated and her eligibility determined
    C. her application will be investigated but if her home is not cleaned up when you visit next week, her application will be rejected
    D. if found eligible for aid to dependent children, she must take instruction in housekeeping from the social services center home economist

8. One of your clients finds it necessary to be away from home for two weeks and arranges with her mother to care for her children, for whom she receives an aid to dependent children grant, without notifying your department about this plan. You discover her absence, however, when making a periodic revisit to the client's apartment.
In view of these facts it would be MOST advisable to   8.____

    A. stop the grant immediately inasmuch as you are unable to see the client at this time
    B. let the grant continue, as the temporary planned absence of the client does not affect her eligibility

C. tell the client's mother that a recipient of aid to dependent children may not leave her children even for a temporary period

D. order the client's mother to wire her to return within two days or the grant will stop

9. When a relief recipient requests that the Department of Social Services take some action because her unemployed husband is indifferent to her and unconcerned about the welfare of their children, the social service worker should   9.____

A. inform the husband that he will be cut out of the grant if he does not change his attitude

B. advise the woman to separate and try to build a life apart from her husband

C. tell the woman to appeal to the Domestic Relations Court to have her husband ordered to spend his evenings at home

D. suggest that the woman discuss this matter with a private family agency

10. A woman appears at your social services center and asks for advice on what to do as she would like, if possible, to be able to remain at home with her three children, aged four, seven, and ten. She declares that her husband has been killed and she is unable to manage on her old age and survivors insurance.
Assuming the facts to be true as stated, the social service worker should advise her   10.____

A. to apply for aid to dependent children

B. to try to find a job

C. to apply for more money under old age and survivors insurance

D. that there are no other public financial resources available in her case

11. A child born out of wedlock to a certain Miss Smith has been placed in a private foster home. Miss Smith is unable to pay anything toward the child's care and one day, in discussing the case with a worker at the Bureau of Child Welfare, she asks about visiting her little girl.
The MOST desirable reply for the social service worker to make in this situation would be that Miss Smith   11.____

A. cannot visit the child because she would exert an adverse influence over her

B. should not visit since she is not paying for the child's care

C. should not visit because it will be difficult for the child to explain to her friends that her mother is unmarried

D. has the same right as any other mother to visit her child

12. Eight-year-old Johnny, on whose account his mother is receiving aid to dependent children, is beginning to truant from school. Disturbed by the course of events, his mother appears at the social services center and informs you, her social service worker, that her efforts to stop Johnny's truancy have been unavailing. You should tell Johnny's mother that   12.____

A. the grant will be discontinued since Johnny's truancy is evidence of her failure as a parent

B. she can be referred to a specialized agency in the community

C. you will institute court action to remove Johnny from his home environment
D. you will give her two months to straighten out the problem before taking further action

13. Suppose you, as social service worker, are considering institutional care for several different types of children for whom removal from present homes is indicated.
Of the following, the type LEAST suited for such care would be   13._____

   A. a child needing observation, study, and treatment for a severe crippling condition
   B. a 15-year-old boy who resents adult authority
   C. a family of six brothers and sisters who are devoted to each other
   D. a normal 3-year-old girl whose mother is dead and whose father is employed at night

14. It is generally agreed among psychologists that children need to have certain experiences in order to develop into healthy, well-integrated adults.
Of the following, it is MOST important to the development of the preadolescent child that he   14._____

   A. live in a good neighborhood
   B. have a room of his own
   C. have nice clothes
   D. have the feeling that he is loved and wanted by his parents

15. The only educative agency which can properly be thought of as really starting with a *clean slate* in developing a person's behavior is the   15._____

   A. family   B. play group
   C. church group   D. elementary school

16. The LEAST accurate of the following statements regarding intelligence is that   16._____

   A. a person's intelligence is not directly related to biological factors
   B. persons differ radically in the degree of intelligence which they have
   C. persons cannot learn beyond the limits of their native intelligence regardless of the amount and kind of effort they expend
   D. ill health, isolation, and certain kinds of temperament may seriously limit the proportion of one's intelligence which he may actually be able to put to use

17. The GREATEST limitation on the general effectiveness of marriage courses in college curricula is   17._____

   A. there is no evidence to prove that such courses result in better matings and happier homes
   B. successful completion of such courses is no indication that the knowledge contained in the courses will be successfully applied by the students who have taken them
   C. there is no complete agreement as to whether the family, the church, or the school should be responsible for guiding marriage education
   D. most of the people who marry are ineligible to enroll in such courses

18. In the following instances, cooperative behavior which results from loyalty to the same objective is BEST exemplified by   18.____

    A. the citizens of a community forming a committee for the purpose of building a school
    B. employer and employee agreeing to a conference for the purpose of arriving at an equitable wage settlement
    C. people attending a championship tennis match held for charitable purposes
    D. the citizens of a German community accepting employment in the local headquarters of the American Military Government

19. Among persons handicapped by blindness, the ones who may be expected to display a range of experience MOST comparable with that of normal persons are those who   19.____

    A. receive no special consideration from others
    B. are closely protected by their kinsmen and friends against the severe limitations imposed by their handicap
    C. are urged to greater attainments than would be expected of normal persons in order to compensate for their affliction
    D. are urged to understand their potentialities and limitations and are encouraged to make the most of their opportunities

20. From the social service point of view, the MOST desirable requisite for a potential social service worker to have at the outset is   20.____

    A. a desire to return full value for the taxpayer's dollar
    B. knowledge of eligibility requirements for relief
    C. understanding of the functions of the Department of Social Services
    D. a desire to help people meet their problems

21. From the case history on a client described as a delinquent individual, illiterate, shy, regarded by others with annoyance or condescension, who hardly ever engages in group activities and never goes to church, movies, or theater, the social service worker would be justified in forming the conclusion that   21.____

    A. the social isolation is responsible for the delinquency
    B. the delinquency is responsible for the social isolation
    C. both the poverty and isolation are responsible for the delinquency
    D. a single case is insufficient for the inference that social isolation is regularly associated with poverty and delinquency

22. If a repatriated citizen disembarks at the Port of New York in a destitute condition, his relief problem will be handled in the following manner: 22.____

    A. he will be cared for by the Department of Social Services and the Federal Security Agency will reimburse the city in full for the expense involved
    B. he will be cared for by the Department of Social Services and the State Board of Social Welfare will reimburse the city in full for the expense involved
    C. he will be cared for by the Department of Social Services and the State will reimburse the city for 80% of the expense involved
    D. he will be cared for by the Immigration and Naturalization Service without cost to the city

23. Recent census figures consistently show that in the age groups from 55 up, the number   23.____
of foreign-born in the United States is greater than would ordinarily be expected in our
population.
The MOST reliable explanation for this condition is probably that

    A. foreigners tend to outlive native Americans because only the hardier among them
venture to emigrate from their own countries
    B. there are comparatively few young people among the foreign-born because, in
recent years, immigration has been materially reduced
    C. foreign-born children have a shorter life expectancy than native-born children of
foreign or American parents
    D. the number of persons who emigrated from the United States to other countries in
recent years exceeds the number who entered this country in the same period

24. A small town without a hospital is located near a large city which boasts of its excellent   24.____
medical facilities. These facilities are extended liberally to non-residents who come from
adjacent centers which do not have hospitals of their own. If it is shown statistically that
the death rate of the small town is lower compared to that of the large city, the MOST logical inference for the alert social service worker to make is that

    A. small-town life is more healthful than living in a big city
    B. the statistical data have been improperly manipulated
    C. death rates should not be determined by political boundaries
    D. the deaths of non-residents have boosted the death rate of the large city

25. Of the types of mental breakdown listed below, the disorder that ordinarily occurs at the   25.____
MOST advanced age is

    A. cerebral arteriosclerosis   B. neurasthenia
    C. dementia praecox   D. paresis

26. The parole movement for releasing prisoners before the expiration of their sentence, has   26.____
gained headway MOSTLY because of the assumption on the part of the taxpaying public
that

    A. prison officials and parole officers can watch the paroled prisoner closely and help
him adjust himself in the community at the same time
    B. recidivism is greater for persons serving their full sentence
    C. it sends the parolee out with an obligation rather than a score to settle
    D. total costs for prison administration are materially reduced when a large percent-
age of the prison population have their terms of incarceration reduced

27. Among the theories advanced in favor of providing unemployment relief, the one that   27.____
should appear to the social service worker as MOST basic is that

    A. it is the responsibility of the government to provide for those unable to provide for
themselves
    B. people would work for very little and thereby bring down salaries if unemployment
relief were not granted
    C. a wholesome economy can exist only when money is kept circulating
    D. every man has the right to a job

28. During a period of economic adjustment when unemployment is on the rise, the invention   28._____
of a labor-saving device would, in the long run, be economically and culturally

    A. unsound because it would stir up unrest among the organized labor groups
    B. unsound because it would result in accelerating unemployment
    C. sound because the rise of unemployment is a temporary phenomenon while the labor-saving device would add permanent values
    D. sound because it would enable the user to produce more with the small working population still employed

29. Wage rates for women in the United States do not match those for men in many indus-   29._____
tries LARGELY because

    A. women tend to constitute a marginal supply of labor
    B. the social attitude has swung back to the position that *woman's place is in the home*
    C. the organized labor movement has modified its traditional stand regarding *equal pay for equal work*
    D. women do not attain highly responsible positions in the business world as consistently as men

30. The inability of people to obtain employment during a time of economic depression is an   30._____
example of the principle that

    A. anyone who really wants a job can get one if he tries hard enough
    B. the more capable people get jobs when jobs are scarce
    C. at certain times employment is not available for many people irrespective of ability, character, or need
    D. full employment is a thing of the past

KEY (CORRECT ANSWERS)

1.	B	11.	D	21.	D
2.	D	12.	B	22.	A
3.	C	13.	D	23.	B
4.	D	14.	D	24.	D
5.	B	15.	A	25.	A
6.	C	16.	A	26.	A
7.	B	17.	D	27.	A
8.	B	18.	A	28.	C
9.	D	19.	D	29.	D
10.	A	20.	D	30.	C

TEST 3

DIRECTIONS: Each question or incomplete statement is followed by several suggested answers or completions. Select the one that BEST answers the question or completes the statement. *PRINT THE LETTER OF THE CORRECT ANSWER IN THE SPACE AT THE RIGHT.*

1. It is often held that cooperative activity is difficult to achieve because *individuals are basically selfish* and their alleged selfishness makes it difficult, if not possible, to subordinate their individual wills to the collective enterprise.
   The CHIEF factor overlooked in such a conception of the matter is that

   A. there is no necessary discrepancy or conflict between selfishness and cooperation
   B. people do not seek to further their self-interest by competitive activity
   C. competition and cooperation are essentially alike
   D. most successful people are not selfish

   1.____

2. Under the law it is always necessary to establish eligibility for public assistance. While the facts that must be established are clearly defined by law and by policy, the social service worker has a good deal of freedom in his choice of method.
   Of the methods given below for obtaining desired information from applicants for relief, the one considered the BEST interviewing method in social work practice, and therefore recommended to the social service worker is to

   A. work from an outline, asking the questions in the order in which they appear and requiring the applicant to give specific answers
   B. let the applicant tell what he has to say in his own way first, the social service worker then taking responsibility for asking questions on points not covered
   C. tell the applicant all the facts that it is necessary to have, then letting him give the information in any way he chooses
   D. verify all such facts as birth date, income, and past employment before seeing the applicant, then asking the applicant to fill in the remaining gaps when he is interviewed

   2.____

3. Suppose an applicant for relief objects to answering a question regarding his recent employment and asks, *What business is it of yours, young man?*
   As the social service worker conducting the interview, the MOST constructive course of action for you to take under the circumstances would be to

   A. tell the applicant you have no intention of prying into his personal affairs and go on to the next question
   B. refer the applicant to your supervisor
   C. rephrase the question so that only a *Yes* or *No* answer is required
   D. explain why the question is being asked

   3.____

4. Continued contact with relief recipients is maintained by social service workers employed by the Department of Social Services MAINLY because   4.____

    A. changes in relief need to be made in accordance with financial changes in the family situation
    B. many people do not report changes in income promptly
    C. most people do not understand that reports of their earnings are required
    D. the department wishes to see that the relief given is properly used

5. Inasmuch as periodic visits to clients at home are required by the Department of Social Services, according to good case work practice, it is MOST desirable for the social service worker to   5.____

    A. visit without appointment as this gives him a chance to see the person and the house *as they really are* and forestalls changing things to create a different impression
    B. write giving an appointment time as this saves the social worker from visiting when people are not home and helps him to plan his work more efficiently
    C. write suggesting an appointment time so that the client may be prepared for the interview and the social worker uses his time economically
    D. advise all applicants during their first interview that they will be visited periodically but will not be given definite appointments

6. Assuming that careful interpretation has been given but an applicant for public assistance refuses to accede to the necessary procedures to establish his eligibility for aid, the MOST preferable of the following courses of action for you to take would be to   6.____

    A. do nothing further
    B. grant temporary aid in the hope that the applicant will change his mind
    C. try to ascertain why the applicant feels as he does, but to respect his decision if he refuses to change his mind
    D. proceed to check on all the facts possible even though the applicant has not given his permission

7. The PRIMARY purpose in discussing with an applicant the steps in determining his eligibility and the kind of verification of facts which the agency will need is to   7.____

    A. enable the applicant to understand the basis of eligibility and participate in determining it
    B. protect the position of the agency so that there will be no comeback if relief is not granted
    C. give the applicant an opportunity to modify any statement he may have made previously
    D. promote public relations for the agency, since the applicant will tell others how the agency is operating

8. The BEST of the following reasons for which a public social services agency should NOT insist on certain standards of cleanliness as a factor in eligibility to receive relief is that it is generally acknowledged that   8.____

    A. people have a right to decide how they will live, provided their mode of living does not hurt others

46

    B. standards of cleanliness vary so much among people as to make one standard impracticable

    C. a little dirt has never hurt anyone

    D. it would take too much of the social service worker's time to maintain a constant check on this factor

9. When a client receives home relief, he   9.____

    A. gives up the right to manage his money in his own way

    B. is justified in assuming that he has proved his eligibility for relief and is free to use the money according to his best judgment

    C. is limited in spending the money only for expenditures itemized in the agency budget

    D. is obligated to keep an itemized list of his expenditures

10. *The knowledge and understanding of situations and of people attained through social case work may well serve as a basis for sound action and for effective social welfare planning.*   10.____

The MOST logical assumption that the social service worker can draw from the statement made above is that

    A. since social service planning is related to broad social issues and needs, it is unnecessary to consider the individual

    B. the individual is the only unit to be considered in the planning of effective social welfare programs

    C. all social planning should be directed primarily toward the individual and his needs

    D. knowledge of the individual attained through social case work can be effectively utilized in planning a broad social welfare program

11. Of the following, the LEAST valid reason for the maintenance of the case record in public social services administration is to   11.____

    A. furnish reference material for other workers

    B. improve the quality of service to the client

    C. show how the public funds are being expended

    D. reduce the complexities of the case to manageable proportions

12. A public social services agency will lean more on forms than a private agency in the same field of activity because   12.____

    A. forms simplify the recording responsibilities of newly appointed social service workers

    B. public social service records are of the family agency type

    C. the governmental framework requires a greater degree of standardization

    D. more interviews and visits are made in connection with public relief cases

13. *In spite of the need which most of us have of finding rules and procedures to guide us, we must face the difficulty at the outset that there is no such thing as a model case record.*   13.____

Of the following, the BEST justification for this statement is that

    A. records should be written to suit the case

    B. case recording should be patterned after the best models obtainable

C. rules cannot be applied to social case work because each case requires individual treatment

D. the establishment of routine and procedures in social work is an ideal which cannot be realized

14. One of the following disclosures is made regarding an applicant for old age assistance and he is accordingly disqualified to receive the grant requested. In the recommendation submitted by the social services worker, the applicant would be found ineligible because he   14.____

    A. is not a citizen

    B. has $100 in a bank account which he is saving for burial purposes

    C. has three married children and could probably live with one of them

    D. refuses to give information concerning a bank account of $5,000 which had been in his name until four months prior to his application

15. The homemaking center of the Department of Social Services furnishes the service of mother's aides to families for help in caring for their children because of the mother's temporary incapacity or absence. Mother's aides can assume responsibility for such household duties as feeding infants, preparing meals, cleaning the home, etc. They are mature, responsible women with previous homemaking experience who have passed a literacy test and have undergone a thorough physical examination. According to current thinking in the field, for the social service worker assigned in any case where a mother's aide is furnished, to use the mother's aide as a source of obtaining confidential information for the Department of Social Services would be   15.____

    A. advisable; as a result of contact with the family, the mother's aide will have observed many details concerning their daily activities

    B. inadvisable; while the mother's aide will have observed many details concerning the daily activities of the family, she has not been trained to interpret these observations

    C. advisable; the mother's aide has been thoroughly examined as to her ability to perform her duties in the household

    D. inadvisable; the mother's aide has a primary obligation to the family rather than to the Department of Social Services

16. When a family asks the help of the social service worker because they are consistently exceeding their food and clothing allowance, the social service worker should   16.____

    A. use the services of the home economist for consultation on the management problem which has developed

    B. order the family to live within their budget allowance

    C. ignore the situation as it is the family's responsibility to make ends meet

    D. recommend small increases in the food and clothing allowance for this family

17. When a landlord complains to the social service worker that a certain relief recipient has consistently neglected to pay his rent, present case work practice would indicate to the social service worker that he should FIRST   17.____

    A. arrange to discontinue relief payments until he can verify the reasons for the non-payment of rent

B. tell the client to pay his rent within a certain period of time if he does not want his relief discontinued

C. tell the client about the landlord's complaint and inform him the Department of Social Services assumes that rent is an obligation the client is expected to settle directly with his landlord

D. arrange for the landlord to collect his rent at the social services center in the future

Questions 18-23

DIRECTIONS: Questions 18 to 23 inclusive deal with social service allowances of various kinds. Assuming that in the Department of Social Services the allowance schedules shown below are among those included in estimating the needs of relief recipients, use the figures given to determine your answers. All figures are quoted on a monthly basis.

Item	Allowance
Rent	as paid by client
Utilities	$12 per person
Person incidentals	$7 per person

	Adult	Child 13-18	Child under 13
Food	$360	$350	$300
Clothing	90	84	79

18. The Anderson family consisting of father, mother, and four children aged 4,10,15, and 17, is eligible for home relief. The rent is $800 a month. Relief granted on the basis of the above items is given semi-monthly. According to the schedule shown, the proper semi-monthly grant for this family would be   18.____

   A. $1,076   B. $1,427   C. $1,717   D. $3,134

19. Assuming that all the expenditures except rent were reimbursed under the State Welfare Law to the same extent that reimbursements for home relief are now being made to the city, the annual cost to the city for all the items included in the public assistance budget of the Anderson family would be APPROXIMATELY   19.____

   A. $8,400   B. $16,000   C. $24,000   D. $28,000

20. Mrs. Peet is 67 years old and applies for old age assistance. She lives with her widowed niece who has a family of three children. The rent of the apartment is $560 a month. The niece has agreed to pay for the utilities of the whole group and also to give Mrs. Peet some money for personal incidentals, provided that Mrs. Peet can pay one-fifth of the rent. On medical advice, a special diet allowance of $77.20 a month is authorized for Mrs. Peet in addition to the regular food allowance.
The proper monthly grant for Mrs. Peet would be   20.____

   A. $498.80   B. $560.75   C. $639.20   D. $1,006.50

21. Mrs. Scalise applies for relief for herself and her two children aged two and four. Her rent costs $650 a month. She is separated from her husband, who contributes $180 a week by court order. It has also been verified that Mrs. Scalise earns $112 a week doing piece-work at home. Assuming that for budget computation purposes the Department of Social Services considers 4.3 weeks as equivalent to one month, the monthly grant in this case would be   21.____

A. $538.10   B. $659.40   C. $938.00   D. $1,012.20

22. A 36-year-old sightless widower applies for aid to the blind. His rent and utilities are met by relatives with whom he lives. In aid to blind cases, $92 per month is allowed for expenses incident to blindness as a substitute for the personal incidentals item in the schedule printed above.
Under these circumstances, the proper monthly grant would be

22._____

     A. $342.50   B. $537.00   C. $646.50   D. $1,057.50

23. John Burke is 52 years old and needs supplementary home relief. He pays $370 a month for his room and he earns $420 a month doing odd jobs.
Basing your computations on these facts and on the schedule above, you can determine that the proper semi-monthly grant for Mr. Burke would be

23._____

     A. $508.50   B. $369.60   C. $209.50   D. $163.00

24. In attempting to discover whether an applicant for aid to dependent children has had any previous experience as a relief recipient through other social service agencies in the community, the social service worker should

24._____

     A. check the application for such aid with the social service exchange
     B. send the fingerprints of the applicant to the Police Department
     C. consult the latest records of the Department of Social Services
     D. ask the applicant to submit a notarized statement to the effect that such aid has not been received from any other source

25. Mr. Ritter asks the Department of Social Services to place his son, aged five, in a foster home. In a subsequent interview, Mr. Ritter refuses to divulge what sources of income are at his disposal.
As the social service worker trying to obtain this information, you should explain to Mr. Ritter that

25._____

     A. you want to know whether he is seeking placement for his son because he does not want to provide for him financially
     B. part of placement procedure involves determining the extent of financial responsibility parents can continue to assume
     C. if he makes no payment his parental rights will be affected
     D. the frequency of his visits will depend on the amount of support he continues to furnish

26. A woman applying for supplementation of her earnings explains that she earns $300 weekly but that the doctor has advised her to work only four days a week in order to safeguard her health. Under the reduced schedule, her earnings would drop to $200 a week and she would be unable to continue supporting her 62-year-old mother.
Assuming that this information has been duly verified, the woman's request for supplementary relief should be

26._____

     A. granted because she supports her old mother
     B. not granted because she can still manage to work a full week
     C. granted because the reduction of work is necessary to preserve her health
     D. not granted because her mother can get old age assistance

27. Suppose a client whom you are investigating has borrowed $250 in order to purchase an 27.____
evening gown for one of her children who is being graduated from high school. She is
planning to repay the loan at the rate of $10 a week, and presents verification of this
transaction as well as of the purchase.
As a social service worker you would be complying with the BEST case work principles by

    A. telling the client her grant will be reduced in view of her ability to manage on $10
less each week
    B. telling the client that she must never do this again
    C. explaining to the client how her action will make it more difficult for the family to get
along on their limited grant
    D. suggesting that she return the dress and repay the borrowed money in this way

28. Mrs. Rose complains to the social service worker about the inadequacy of her relief 28.____
allowance although she is being granted the maximum amount for a person in her situation. It is acknowledged by the Department of Social Services that the amount of the
grant is not based on current prices.
Under these circumstances, the MOST considerate reply the social service worker can
make to this complainant is that

    A. the grant is based on a scientific calculation of needs for subsistence and is only a
small percentage short of what is actually needed
    B. the social worker knows it is difficult to manage since the cost of living was steadily
rising, but that the amount granted was all the Department of Social Services
schedule allows at the present time
    C. Mrs. Rose would be worse off if there were no public assistance
    D. many people in other countries do not have even the small grant allowed Mrs.
Rose

29. Miss Lowe applies for assistance and is able to account for her work history and her 29.____
financial expenditures with the exception of three months in 1997.
As acting intake interviewer, it would be your responsibility to inform her that

    A. she will remain ineligible until she accounts for her complete work history
    B. her application can be accepted, but that certain verification will have to be made
as to her statements regarding lack of resources
    C. she is obviously hiding pertinent information and that her application cannot there-
fore be considered
    D. she obviously had some sources of help in 1997 and that she should use this
source again

30. Knowing that a client needs a period of rest and that another agency can arrange this, it 30.____
would be the responsibility of a social service worker to

    A. notify the client of this resource and suggest that he apply there if he wishes to
    B. try to make all the arrangements for the client, telling the other agency he knows all
about the client's situation and can apply for him
    C. tell the client that unless he applies to the other agency, he will do so for him
    D. tell the client he seems insufficiently interested in getting well enough to work and
the Department of Social Services may discontinue his assistance

31. An irate citizen comes into the Social Services office protesting that William Case, a relief 31.____
recipient, made no effort to shop most economically and was therefore wasting public
funds which he, a taxpayer, in part contributed. The complainant wants to know why Mr.
Case was given cash instead of a food voucher.
The social service worker should tell this citizen that the Department of Social Services will not transfer Mr. Case to voucher relief because cash relief

   A. is easier to administer
   B. enables the investigator to know how responsible a person is by the way he spends
      his money
   C. enables people to maintain their usual way of living
   D. keeps money in circulation

32. Assume that a certain Mr. Sears applied for relief three weeks ago. As he has not yet 32.____
received any assistance, he comes to see the social service worker to find out why he is
being neglected. A checkup of Mr. Sears' status reveals that his application has been
inactive pending receipt of a reply from a former employer. When informed of this contin-
gency, Mr. Sears offers to expedite matters by getting in touch with the employer himself.
The BEST way for the social service worker to handle this case would be to tell Mr.
Sears that

   A. the determination of his eligibility is the responsibility of the social service worker
      alone
   B. it would help if he could hurry the reply
   C. if he discusses this with the employer, the information will be invalidated
   D. he should just go home and wait

33. When he applies for public relief, a man gives a complete and straightforward account of 33.____
his past employment and earnings, of the inability of his relatives to help, and of his
attempts to find work. The way the family has managed in the past indicates excellent
planning ability in the use of money and making limited resources go a long way. He says
he exhausted all resources before applying, and gives a detailed account. The family
lived on less than a relief allowance while receiving unemployment compensation. They
have exhausted their credit at the grocery store. The landlord is threatening eviction
because of rent arrears of two months. He explains he went through all this because it is
so painful for him to apply for relief. The man is obviously honest and reliable.
Under these circumstances, a conscientious social service worker would find that

   A. it is unnecessary to verify the foregoing information in order to establish eligibility
   B. it is necessary to verify the facts given above in order to establish eligibility
   C. the interviewer should be free to decide whether any verifications are needed
   D. eligibility considerations should be waived and an immediate grant made in order
      to help the man feel better

34. Mr. Russell complains to his social service worker that he is too feeble to cook his own 34.____
food and needs more money in order to eat in restaurants. If investigation of the request
proves that Mr. Russell's condition is as indicated, the social service worker should

   A. explain why no provision can be made for this additional expense
   B. suggest that Mr. Russell get a neighbor to help with the cooking
   C. recommend that the allowance be increased
   D. explain that relief recipients should not eat in restaurants

35. When applying for unemployment relief, a prospective client states that he can get a job   35.____
immediately at $300 a week but that he has hesitated to accept such employment
because he feels his income would be inadequate to support his family which, besides
himself, includes his wife and two children. The applicant also states that he has enrolled
in a training program which, if he can pursue to a satisfactory conclusion two weeks
hence, will enable him to accept a job paying $500 weekly.
If you were the social service worker in this case, the MOST constructive of the following courses of action for you to take would be to

    A. recommend that relief be given immediately
    B. recommend that relief not be given because the applicant has a $300 job available
       to him
    C. tell the applicant he must take the $300 job and then give him supplementation on
       account of his inadequate earnings
    D. recommend relief if the information is verified

————

KEY (CORRECT ANSWERS)

1.	A	11.	D	26.	C
2.	B	12.	C	27.	C
3.	D	13.	A	28.	B
4.	A	14.	D	29.	B
5.	C	15.	B	30.	A
6.	C	16.	A	31.	C
7.	A	17.	C	32.	B
8.	A	18.	C	33.	B
9.	B	19.	B	34.	C
10.	D	20.	C	35.	D
		21.	B		
		22.	B		
		23.	C		
		24.	A		
		25.	B		

————

EXAMINATION SECTION
TEST 1

DIRECTIONS: Each of the following questions consists of a statement. You are to decide whether the statement is true or false. Then, on the answer sheet, alongside the number corresponding to the question, indicate the letter *C* if the statement is true or correct; or indicate the letter *W* if the statement is false or wrong.

1. The social service worker often finds it necessary to get in touch with numerous sources of information in order to verify a client's eligibility for public assistance, but the primary source of information regarding a client is usually the client himself.

1.____

2. A social service worker can MOST readily establish an effective relationship with his clients by showing great solicitude for their welfare and assuring them of his anxiety to *do things* for them.

2.____

3. One of the MOST important factors contributing to the potential success of a plan worked out to resolve the difficulties faced by a client of the Department of Social Services, is the client's approval.

3.____

4. The PRIMARY purpose of a case record is to provide a detailed statement regarding the activities of the case worker for the use of the case supervisor.

4.____

5. As used in social case work, *referral* and *transfer* are synonymous terms.

5.____

6. In a large city, home visits must be made to recipients of public assistance at least once every three months regardless of the type of assistance being given.

6.____

7. Home relief may not be granted to an individual in a public institution.

7.____

8. In general, the settlement of a married woman is that of her husband.

8.____

9. A person must be a citizen of the United States in order to qualify for old age assistance.

9.____

10. An elderly person who wishes to attend a day care center for the aged, which is maintained under Department of Social Services supervision, MUST promise to attend regularly.

10.____

11. If primary sources of proof of age are not available, the age of an applicant for old age assistance may be determined by affidavits of reliable and disinterested persons.

11.____

12. Public assistance in the form of aid to the blind may not be granted to any person who solicits alms.

12.____

13. A special requirement for receiving assistance to the blind on a continuing basis is a classification of blindness, as defined by the Social Welfare Law, made by the State Commission for the Blind.

13.____

14. If a client's landlord complains that the client is delinquent in rent payments, and the case record shows that money for this purpose was provided by the Department of Social Services, the social service worker should recommend that assistance to this client be immediately discontinued.

14.____

15. The Department of Social Services is not intended by law to render psychiatric treat-ment.

15.____

16. Examination by a psychiatrist should be recommended only when a client is thought to be suffering from some form of insanity.

16.____

17. The intelligence quotient is a reliable index of a person's character and personality.

17.____

18. The social service worker is responsible for determining the total available resources of each member of an applicant's family.

18.____

19. The social service worker plans budgets for the families in his case load mainly because analysis of the figures enables him to advise the members of these families how to spend their allowances.

19.____

20. When a presumably destitute woman informs a social service worker that she is liable to become a public charge although she has a well-to-do brother who refuses to offer her any financial assistance, the worker should institute proceedings to compel the brother to undertake financial responsibility.

20.____

21. When an applicant asks a social service worker only for financial assistance for himself and his family, the worker should assume that the applicant has no need of any other ser-vices of the Department of Social Services.

21.____

22. The homemaker's service of the Department of Social Services may be furnished to a family not receiving public assistance.

22.____

23. Any person who receives an income from pension payments is not eligible for public assistance under the Social Welfare Law.

23.____

24. Geriatrics is that branch of medical science which is concerned with the treatment of chil-dren's diseases.

24.____

25. When a relief recipient is found to be employable, he may under certain circumstances be permitted to remain on the relief rolls even though he refuses to accept a job offer.

25.____

26. When the Social Security Act was amended recently, eligibility for social security benefits was extended to all employees of charitable organizations on the same basis as to household employees.

26.____

27. Aid to dependent children may be granted to unmarried mothers for their children born out of wedlock.

27.____

28. It is a function of the Department of Social Services to investigate complaints alleging neglect of children who have been placed, at public expense, in foster care.

28.____

29. Under the Social Welfare Law, a stepfather would be held legally responsible for the sup-port of his minor stepchildren.

29.____

30. The application of an 18-year-old married daughter of a veteran should be accepted for veteran assistance on the basis of her father's veteran status.

30.____

KEY (CORRECT ANSWERS)

1.	C	11.	C	21.	W
2.	W	12.	C	22.	C
3.	C	13.	C	23.	W
4.	W	14.	W	24.	W
5.	W	15.	C	25.	C
6.	W	16.	W	26.	W
7.	C	17.	W	27.	C
8.	C	18.	C	28.	C
9.	W	19.	W	29.	C
10.	W	20.	W	30.	W

TEST 2

DIRECTIONS: Each of the following questions consists of a statement. You are to decide whether the statement is true or false. Then, on the answer sheet, alongside the number corresponding to the question, indicate the letter C if the statement is true or correct; or indicate the letter W if the statement is false or wrong

1. A Department of Social Services client who is eligible for veteran assistance may not receive any other form of public-assistance from the Department of Social Services.   1.____

2. It is generally preferable to place a dependent child in a foster home rather than in an institution.   2.____

3. Assistance in the form of aid to dependent children is provided on the assumption that children are better off with their mothers regardless of the circumstances.   3.____

4. The CHIEF reason for committing deliquent children to an institution is to protect other children from the influence of evil companions.   4.____

5. A resident of the state would lose his state residence under the Social Welfare Law by removal and absence from the state for a period of six months.   5.____

6. Inhabitants of Puerto Rico acquired American citizenship in 1917.   6.____

7. The suffrage in Puerto Rico is restricted to men.   7.____

8. The Governor of Puerto Rico is elected by the people of Puerto Rico.   8.____

9. United States currency is used EXCLUSIVELY in Puerto Rico.   9.____

10. The share of Puerto Rico tax revenues devoted to education is severely limited in comparison with the proportion of tax funds devoted to education by states on the mainland of the United States.   10.____

11. The excise tax on a bottle of Puerto Rican rum purchased in this city would ultimately go to the Government of Puerto Rico and not to the United States Treasury.   11.____

12. According to the latest available census figures, the population of Puerto Rico is between one and a half million and two million.   12.____

13. Puerto Rico has an average density of about 225 persons per square mile as compared to 47 persons in the United States.   13.____

14. The vast majority of the migrant Puerto Ricans who come to this city are from urban centers in Puerto Rico.   14.____

15. More than 75% of the population of Puerto Rico are within the age group of 35 and under.   15.____

16. The reduction of the death rate in Puerto Rico has been accompanied by a corresponding reduction in the birth rate. 16.____

17. The migration stream of Puerto Ricans coming to New York includes a greater proportion of women than of men. 17.____

18. The percentage of illiteracy in Puerto Rico is at present about 50%. 18.____

19. The Puerto Ricans who come to this city are in general more illiterate than those who remain on the island. 19.____

20. Over 10,000 Puerto Ricans work in hotels and restaurants. 20.____

21. An excess of exports over merchandise imports has been characteristic of the Puerto Rican economy for the past ten years. 21.____

22. The percentage of the labor force engaged in farming in Puerto Rico has declined in comparison with the farm labor force of a generation ago. 22.____

23. Much of the economic assistance Puerto Rico gets from the United States is administered under the auspices of the Point Four program. 23.____

24. Puerto Rico does NOT supply its own food needs. 24.____

25. Codfish is the PRINCIPAL source of protein for Puerto Rico. 25.____

26. On the entire island of Puerto Rico, there is NOT one municipality without standard electric current. 26.____

27. Government lotteries, though common in many Spanish-speaking countries, are NOT permitted in Puerto Rico. 27.____

28. The children of Puerto Rico traditionally receive gifts on Three Kings Day instead of on Christmas. 28.____

29. The word *grifo* is associated with the history of fine arts in Puerto Rico. 29.____

30. A type of folk tune that corresponds to the American ballad is known as the *danza*. 30.____

———

KEY (CORRECT ANSWERS)

1.	W	11.	C	21.	W
2.	C	12.	W	22.	C
3.	W	13.	W	23.	W
4.	W	14.	C	24.	C
5.	W	15.	C	25.	C
6.	C	16.	W	26.	C
7.	W	17.	C	27.	W
8.	C	18.	W	28.	C
9.	C	19.	W	29.	W
10.	W	20.	C	30.	W

EXAMINATION SECTION
TEST 1

DIRECTIONS : Each question or incomplete statement is followed by several suggested answers or completions. Select the one that *BEST* answers the question or completes the statement. *PRINT THE LETTER OF THE CORRECT ANSWER IN THE SPACE AT THE RIGHT.*

1. When a worker is planning a future interview with a client, of the following, the *MOST* important consideration is the

    A. recommendations he will make to the client
    B. place where the client will be interviewed
    C. purpose for which the client will be interviewed
    D. personality of the client

1.____

2. For a worker to make a practice of reviewing the client's case record, if available, prior to the interview, is usually

    A. *inadvisable,* because knowledge of the client's past record will tend to influence the worker's judgment
    B. *advisable,* because knowledge of the client's back-ground will help the worker to identify discrepancies in the client's responses
    C. *inadvisable,* because such review is time-consuming and of questionable value
    D. *advisable,* because knowledge of the client's back-ground will help the worker to understand the client's situation

2.____

3. Assume that a worker makes a practice of constantly re-assuring clients with serious and complex problems by making such statements as: *I'm sure you'll soon be well; I know you'll get a job soon;* or *Everything will be all right.*
    Of the following, the *most likely* result of such a practice is to

    A. encourage the client and make him feel that the worker understands what the client is going through
    B. make the client doubtful about the worker's understanding of his difficulties and the worker's ability to help
    C. confuse the client and cause him to hesitate to take any action on his own initiative
    D. help the client to be more realistic about his situation and the probability that it will improve

3.____

4. In order to get the maximum amount of information from a client during an interview, of the following, it is *MOST* important for the worker to communicate to the client the feeling that the worker is

    A. interested in the client
    B. a figure of authority
    C. efficient in his work habits
    D. sympathetic to the client's life style

4.____

5. Of the following, the worker who takes extremely detailed notes during an interview with a client is *most likely* to

    5.____

    A. encourage the client to talk freely
    B. distract and antagonize the client
    C. help the client feel at ease
    D. understand the client's feelings

6. You find that many of the clients you interview are verbally abusive and unusually hostile to you.
Of the following, the *most appropriate* action for you to take *FIRST* is to

    6.____

    A. review your interviewing techniques and consider whether you may be provoking these clients
    B. act in a more authoritative manner when interviewing troublesome clients
    C. tell these clients that you will not process their applications unless their troublesome behavior ceases
    D. disregard the clients' troublesome behavior during the interviews

7. During an interview, you did not completely understand several of your client's responses. In each instance, you rephrased the client's statement and asked the client if that was what he meant.
For you to use such a technique during interviews would be considered

    7.____

    A. *inappropriate;* you may have distorted the client's meaning by rephrasing his statements
    B. *inappropriate;* you should have asked the same question until you received a comprehensible response
    C. *appropriate;* the client will have a chance to correct you if you have misinterpreted his responses
    D. *appropriate;* a worker should rephrase clients' responses for the records

8. A worker is interviewing a client who has just had a severe emotional shock because of an assault on her by a mugger.
Of the following, the approach which would generally be *most helpful* to the client is for the worker to

    8.____

    A. comfort the client and encourage her to talk about the assault
    B. sympathize with the client but refuse to discuss the assault with her
    C. tell the client to control her emotions and think positively about the future
    D. proceed with the interview in an impersonal and un-emotional manner

9. A worker finds that her questions are misinterpreted by many of the clients she interviews.
Of the following, the *most likely* reason for this problem is that the

    9.____

    A. client is not listening attentively
    B. client wants to avoid the subject being discussed
    C. worker has failed to express her meaning clearly
    D. worker has failed to put the client at ease

10. For a worker to look directly at the client and observe him during the interview is, gener-   10.____
ally,

    A. *inadvisable;* this will make the client nervous and uncomfortable
    B. *advisable;* the client will be more likely to refrain from lying
    C. *inadvisable;* the worker will not be able to take notes for the case record
    D. *advisable;* this will encourage conversation and accelerate the progress of the
       interview

11. You are interviewing a client who is applying for social services for the first time.   11.____
In order to encourage this client to freely give you the information needed for you to
establish his eligibility, of the following, the *BEST* way to *start* the interview is by

    A. asking questions the client can easily answer
    B. conveying the impression that his responses to your questions will be checked
    C. asking two or three similar but important questions
    D. assuring the client that your sole responsibility is *getting the facts*

12. Workers are encouraged to record significant information obtained from clients and ser-   12.____
vices provided for clients. Of the following, the *MOST* important reason for this practice is
that these case records will

    A. help to reduce the need for regular supervisory conferences
    B. indicate to workers which clients are taking up the most time
    C. provide information which will help the agency to improve its services to clients
    D. make it easier to verify the complaints of clients

13. As a worker in the employment eligibility section, you find that interviews can be com-   13.____
pleted in a shorter period of time if you ask questions which limit the client to a certain
answer.
For you to use such a technique would be considered

    A. *inappropriate,* because this type of question usually requires advance preparation
    B. *inappropriate,* because this type of question may inhibit the client from saying what
       he really means
    C. *appropriate,* because you know the areas into which the questions should be
       directed
    D. *appropriate,* because this type of question usually helps clients to express them-
       selves clearly

14. Assume that a worker at a juvenile detention center is planning foster care placement for a child.
For the worker to have the child participate in the planning is generally considered to be

    A. time-consuming and of little practical value in preparing the child for placement
    B. valuable in helping the child adjust to future placement
    C. useful, because the child will be more likely to cooperate with others in the center
    D. anxiety-provoking, because the child will feel that he has been abandoned

14.____

15. You have been assigned to interview the mother of a five-year-old son in her home to get information useful in locating the child's absent father. During the interview, you notice many serious bruises on the child's arms and legs, which the mother explains are due to the child's clumsiness.
Of the following, your BEST course of action is to

    A. accept the mother's explanation and concentrate on getting information which will help you to locate the father
    B. advise the mother to have the child examined for a medical condition that may be causing his clumsiness
    C. make a surprise visit to the mother later, to see whether someone is beating the child
    D. complete your interview with the mother and report the case to your supervisor for investigation of possible child abuse

15.____

16. During an interview, the former landlord of an absent father offers to help you to locate the father if you will give the landlord confidential information you have on the financial situation of the father.
Of the following, you should

    A. immediately end the interview with the landlord
    B. urge the landlord to help you but explain that you are not permitted to give him confidential information
    C. freely give the landlord the confidential information he requests about the father
    D. give the landlord the information only if he promises to keep it confidential

16.____

17. You feel that your client, a released mental patient, is not adjusting well to living on his own in an apartment. To gather more information, you interview privately his next-door neighbor, who claims that the client is creating a *disturbance* and speaks of the client in an angry and insulting manner.
Of the following, the BEST action for you to take in this situation is to

    A. listen patiently to the neighbor to try to get the facts about your client's behavior
    B. inform the neighbor that he has no right to speak insultingly about a mentally ill person
    C. make an appointment to interview the neighbor some other time when he isn't so upset
    D. tell the neighbor that you were not aware of the client's behavior and that you will have the client moved

17.____

18. As a worker assigned to an income maintenance center, you are interviewing a client to determine his elibility for a work program. Suddenly the client begins to shout that he is in no condition to work and that you are persecuting him for no reason.
Of the following, your *BEST* response to this client is to

    A. advise the client to stop shouting or you will call for the security guard
    B. wait until the client calms down, then order him to come back for another interview
    C. insist that you are not persecuting the client and that he must complete the inter-view
    D. wait until the client calms down, say that you understand how he feels, and try to continue the interview

18.____

19. You are counseling a mother whose 17-year-old son has recently been returned home from a mental institution. Although she is willing to care for her son at home, she is frightened by his strange and sometimes violent behavior and does not know the best arrangement to make for his care.
Of the following, your *MOST* appropriate response to this mother's problem is to

    A. describe the supportive services and alternatives to home care which are available
    B. help her to accept her son's strange and violent behavior
    C. tell her that she will not be permitted to care for her son at home if she is frightened by his behavior
    D. convince her that she is not responsible for her son's mental condition

19.____

20. Assume that, as an intake worker, you are interviewing an elderly man who comes to the center several times a month to discuss topics with you which are not related to social services. You realize that the man is lonely and enjoys these conversations.
Of the following, it would be *MOST* appropriate to

    A. politely discourage the man from coming in to pass the time with you
    B. avoid speaking to this man the next time he comes into the center
    C. explore with the client his feelings about joining a Senior Citizens' Center
    D. continue to hold these conversations with the man

20.____

21. A client you are interviewing in the housing elibility section tends to ramble on after each response that he gives, so that many clients are kept waiting.
In this situation, of the following, it would be *MOST* advisable to

    A. try to direct the interview, in order to obtain the necessary information
    B. reduce the number of questions asked so that you can shorten the interview
    C. arrange a second interview for the client so that you can give him more time
    D. tell the client that he is wasting everybody's time

21.____

22. A non-minority worker in an employment eligibility unit is about to interview a minority client on public assistance for job placement when the client says: *What does your kind know about my problems? You've never had to survive out on these streets.* Of the following, the worker's *MOST* appropriate response in this situation is to

    A. postpone the interview until a minority worker is available to interview the client
    B. tell the client that he must cooperate with the worker if he wants to continue receiving public assistance
    C. explain to the client the function of the worker in this unit and the services he provides
    D. assure the client that you do not have to be a member of a minority group to understand the effects of poverty

22.____

23. As a worker in a family services unit, you have been assigned to follow-up a case folder recently forwarded from the protective-diagnostic unit. After making appropriate clerical notations in your records such as name of client and date of receipt, which of the following would be the *MOST* appropriate step to take *next*?

    A. Confer with your supervisor
    B. Read and review all reports included in the case folder
    C. Arrange to visit with the client at his home
    D. Confer with representatives of any other agencies which have been in contact with the client

23.____

24. As a worker in the employment section, you are interviewing a young client who seriously underestimates the amount of education and training he will require for a certain occupation. For you to tell the client that you think he is mistaken would, generally, be considered

    A. *inadvisable,* because workers should not express their opinions to clients
    B. *inadvisable,* because clients have the right to self-determination
    C. *advisable,* because clients should generally be alerted to their misconceptions
    D. *advisable,* because workers should convince clients to adopt a proper life style

24.____

25. As an intake worker, you are counseling a mother and her unmarried, thirteen-year-old daughter, who is six months pregnant, concerning the advisability of placing the daughter's baby for adoption. The mother insists on adoption, but the daughter remains silent and appears undecided. Of the following, you should encourage the daughter to

    A. make the final decision on adoption herself
    B. keep her baby despite her mother's insistence on adoption
    C. accept her mother's insistence on adoption
    D. make the decision on adoption together with her mother

25.____

KEY (CORRECT ANSWERS)

1.	C	11.	A
2.	D	12.	C
3.	B	13.	B
4.	A	14.	B
5.	B	15.	D
6.	A	16.	B
7.	C	17.	A
8.	A	18.	D
9.	C	19.	A
10.	D	20.	C

21.	A
22.	C
23.	B
24.	C
25.	D

TEST 2

DIRECTIONS: Each question or incomplete statement is followed by several suggested answers or completions. Select the one that *BEST* answers the question or completes the statement. *PRINT THE LETTER OF THE CORRECT ANSWER IN THE SPACE AT THE RIGHT.*

1. You are interviewing a legally responsible absent father who refuses to make child support payments because he claims the mother physically abuses the child. Of the following, the *BEST* way for you to handle this situation is to tell the father that you

   A. will report his complaint about the mother, but he is still responsible for making child support payments
   B. suspect that he is complaining about the mother in order to avoid his own responsibility for making child support payments
   C. are concerned with his responsibility to make child support payments, not with the mother's abuse of the child
   D. can not determine his responsibility for making child support payments until his complaint about the mother is investigated

1.____

2. On a visit to a home where child abuse is alleged, you find the mother preparing lunch for her two children. She tells you that she knows that a neighbor is spreading lies about her treatment of the children.
   Which one of the following is the *BEST* action for you to take?

   A. Thank the mother for her assistance, leave the home, and indicate in your report that the allegation of child abuse is false
   B. Tell the mother that, since you have been sent to visit her, there must be some truth to the allegations
   C. Explain the purpose of your visit and observe whatever interaction takes place between the children and the mother
   D. Conclude the interview, since you have observed the mother preparing a good lunch for the children

2.____

3. You are interviewing an elderly woman who lives alone to determine her eligibility for homemaker service at public expense. Though obviously frail and in need of this service, the woman is not completely cooperative, and,during the interview, is often silent for a considerable period of time.
   Of the following, the *BEST* way for you to deal with these periods of silence is to

   A. realize that she may be embarrassed to have to apply for homemaker service at public expense, and emphasize her right to this service
   B. postpone the interview and make an appointment with her for a later date, when she may be better able to cooperate
   C. explain to the woman that you have many clients to interview and need her cooperation to complete the interview quickly
   D. recognize that she is probably hiding something and begin to ask questions to draw her out

3.____

4. During a conference with an adolescent boy at a juvenile detention center, you find out for the first time that he would prefer to be placed in foster care rather than return to his natural parents.
    To uncover the reasons why the boy dislikes his own home, of the following, it would be *MOST* advisable for you to

    A. ask the boy a number of short, simple questions about his feelings
    B. encourage the boy to talk freely and express his feelings as best he can
    C. interview the parents and find out why the boy doesn't want to live at home
    D. administer a battery of psychological tests in order to make an assessment of the boy's problems

4._____

5. Of the following, the *BEST* way to determine which activities should be provided for members of a Senior Citizens' Center is to

    A. ask the neighborhood community board to submit their recommendations
    B. meet with the professional staff of the center to get their opinions
    C. encourage the members of the center to express their personal preferences
    D. study the schedules prepared by other Senior Citizens' Centers for guidance

5._____

6. You are interviewing a mother who is applying for Aid to Families with Dependent Children because the husband has deserted the family. The mother becomes annoyed at having to answer your questions and tells you to leave her apartment. Which one of the following actions would be *most appropriate* to take *FIRST* in this situation?

    A. Return to the office and close the case for lack of cooperation
    B. Tell the mother that you will get the information from her neighbors if she does not cooperate
    C. Tell the mother that you must stay until you get answers to your questions
    D. Explain to the mother the reasons for the interview and the consequences of her failure to cooperate

6._____

7. A worker assigned to visit homebound clients to determine their eligibility for Medicaid must understand each client's situation as completely as possible.
    Of the following sources which may provide insight into the client's situation, the *one* that is generally *MOST* revealing is:

    A. Close relatives of the client, who have known him for many years
    B. Next-door neighbors, who have observed the daily living habits of the client
    C. The client himself, who can provide his own description of his situation
    D. The records of other social service agencies that may have served the client

7._____

8. A worker counseling juvenile clients finds that, although he can tolerate most of their behavior, he becomes infuriated when they lie to him.
    Of the following, the worker can *BEST* deal with his anger at his clients' lying by

    A. recognizing his feelings of anger and learning to control expression of these feelings to his clients
    B. warning his clients that he cannot be responsible for his anger when a client lies to him
    C. using will power to suppress his feelings of anger when a client lies to him
    D. realizing that lying is a common trait of juveniles and not directed against him personally

8._____

9. During an interview at the employment eligibility section, one of your clients, a former drug addict, has expressed an interest in attending a community counseling center and resuming his education.
    In this case, the *most appropriate* action that you should take *FIRST* is to

    A. determine whether this ambition is realistic for a former drug addict
    B. send the client's application to a community counseling center which provides services to former addicts
    C. ask the client whether he is really motivated or is just seeking your approval
    D. encourage and assist the client to take this step, since his interest is a positive sign

9._____

10. Because of habitual neglect by his mother, a five-year-old boy has been placed in a foster home.
    For the worker to encourage the mother to visit the boy in the foster home is, generally,

    A. *desirable,* because the boy will be helped by continuing his ties with his mother during the separation
    B. *undesirable,* because the boy will be upset by his mother's visits and will have a harder time adjusting to the foster home
    C. *desirable,* because the mother will learn from the foster parents how she should treat the boy
    D. *undesirable,* because the mother should be punished for her neglect of the boy by complete separation from him

10._____

11. You are interviewing a client who, during previous appointments, has not responded to your requests for information required to determine his continued eligibility for services. On this occasion, the client again offers an excuse which you feel is not acceptable.
    For you to advise the client of the probable loss of services because of his lack of cooperation is

    A. *inappropriate,* because the threat to withhold services will harm the relationship between worker and client
    B. *inappropriate,* because workers should not reveal to clients that they do not believe their statements
    C. *appropriate,* because social services are a reward given to cooperative clients
    D. *appropriate,* because the worker should inform clients of the consequences of their lack of cooperation

11._____

12. Assume that you are counseling an adolescent boy in a juvenile detention center who   12.____
has been a ringleader in smuggling *pot* into the center.
During your regular interview with this boy, of the following, it would be *advisable* to

    A. tell him you know that he has been involved in smuggling pot and that you are try-ing to understand the reasons for his misbehavior

    B. ignore his pot smuggling in order to reassure him that you understand and accept him, even though you do not agree with his standards of behavior

    C. warn him that you have reported his pot smuggling and that he will be punished for his misbehavior

    D. show him that you disapprove of his pot smuggling, but assure him that you will not report him for his misbehavior

13. Your unit has received several complaints about a homeless elderly woman living out-   13.____
doors in various locations in the area. To help determine the need for protective services for this woman, you interview several persons in the neighborhood who are familiar with her, but all are uncooperative or reluctant to give information.
Of the following, your *BEST* approach to these persons is to explain to them that

    A. you will take legal steps against them if they do not cooperate with you

    B. their cooperation may enable you to help this homeless woman

    C. you need their cooperation to remove this homeless woman from their neighbor-hood

    D. they will be responsible for any harm that comes to this homeless woman

14. A foster mother complains to the worker that a ten-year-old boy placed with her is over-   14.____
aggressive and unmanageable. The worker, knowing that the boy has been placed unsuccessfully several times before, constantly reassures the foster mother that the boy is improving steadily.
For the worker to do this is, generally,

    A. *good practice,* because the foster mother may accept the professional opinion of the worker and keep the boy

    B. *poor practice,* because the foster mother may be discouraged from discussing the boy's problems with the worker

    C. *good practice,* because the foster mother may feel guilty if she gives up the boy when he is improving

    D. *poor practice,* because the boy should not remain with a foster mother who com-plains about his behavior

15. Assume that, as a worker in the liaison and adjustment unit, you are interviewing a client   15.____
regarding an adjustment in budget. The client begins to scream at you that she holds you responsible for the decrease in her allowance. Of the following, which is the *BEST* way for you to handle this situation?

    A. Attempt to discuss the matter calmly with the client and explain her right to a hear-ing

    B. Urge the client to appeal and assure her of your support

    C. Tell the client that her disorderly behavior will be held against her

    D. Tell the client that the reduction is *due to red tape* and is not your fault

16. As a worker assigned to a juvenile detention center, you are having a counseling inter-   16.____
    view with a recently admitted boy who is having serious problems in adjusting to confine-
    ment in the center. During the interview, the boy frequently interrupts to ask you personal
    questions.
    Of the following, the *BEST* way for you to deal with these questions is to

    A. tell him in a friendly way that your job is to discuss his problems, not yours
    B. try to understand how the questions relate to the boy's own problems and reply
       with discretion
    C. take no notice of the questions and continue with the interview
    D. try to win the boy's confidence by answering his questions in detail

17. A worker is interviewing an elderly woman who hesitates to provide necessary informa-   17.____
    tion about her finances to determine whether she is eligible for supplementary assis-
    tance. She fears that this information will be reported to others and that her neighbors
    will find out that she is destitute and applying for *welfare*.
    Of the following, the worker's *MOST* appropriate response is to

    A. tell her that, if she hesitates to give this information, the agency will get it from
       other sources
    B. assure her that this information is kept strictly confidential and will not be given to
       unauthorized persons
    C. convince her that her application will be turned down unless she provides this infor-
       mation as soon as possible
    D. ask for the name and address of her nearest relative and obtain the information
       from that person

18. You are counseling a couple whose children have been placed in a foster home because   18.____
    of the couple's quarreling and child neglect. When you interview the wife by herself, she
    tells you that she knows the husband often *cheats* on her with other women, but she is
    too afraid of the husband's temper to tell him how much this hurts her. For you to imme-
    diately reveal to the husband the wife's unhappiness concerning his *cheating* is, gener-
    ally,

    A. *good practice,* because it will help the husband to understand why his wife quarrels
       with him
    B. *poor practice,* because information received from the wife should not be given to
       the husband without her permission
    C. *good practice,* because the husband will direct his anger at you rather than at his
       wife
    D. *poor practice,* because the wife may have told you a false story about her husband
       in order to win your sympathy

19. A worker in an employment eligibility section is beginning a job placement interview with a tall, strongly-built young man. As the man sits down, the worker comments: *I know a big fellow like you wouldn't be interested in any clerical job.*
For the worker to make such a comment is, generally,

19.____

    A. *appropriate,* because it creates an air of familiarity which may put the man at ease
    B. *inappropriate,* because the man may be sensitive about his physical size
    C. *appropriate,* because the worker is using his judgment to help speed up the interview
    D. *inappropriate,* because the man may feel he is being pressured into agreeing with the worker

20. Workers at a juvenile detention center are responsible for establishing constructive relationships with the youths confined to the center in order to help them adjust to detention. Of the following, the *BEST* way for a worker to deal with a youth who acts over-aggressive and hostile is to

20.____

    A. take appropriate disciplinary measures
    B. attempt to distract the youth by encouraging him to engage in physical sports
    C. try to discover the real reasons for the youth's hostile behavior
    D. urge the youth to express his anger against the institution instead of *taking it out* on you

21. A worker in a men's shelter is counseling a middle-aged client for alcoholism. During counseling, the client confesses that, many years ago, he had often enjoyed sexually abusing his ten-year-old daughter. The worker tells the client that he personally finds the client's behavior *morally disgusting.* For the worker to tell the client this is, generally,

21.____

    A. *acceptable counseling practice,* because it may encourage the client to feel guilty about his behavior
    B. *unacceptable counseling practice,* because the client may try to shock the worker by confessing other similar behavior
    C. *acceptable counseling practice,* because *letting off steam* in this manner may relieve tension between the worker and the client
    D. *unacceptable counseling practice,* because the client may hesitate to discuss his behavior frankly with the worker in the future

22. During your discussion with a foster mother who has had a nine-year-old boy in placement for about one month, you are told that the child is disruptive in school and has been unruly and hostile toward the foster family. The boy had been quiet and docile before placement.
In this situation, it would be *MOST* appropriate to suggest to the foster mother that

22.____

    A. this behavior is normal for a nine-year-old boy
    B. children placed in foster homes usually go through a period of testing their foster parents
    C. the child must have picked up these patterns from the foster family
    D. this behavior is probably a sign that she is too strict with the boy

23. During an interview in the housing eligibility section, your client, who wants to move to a larger apartment, asks you to decide on a suitable neighborhood for her. For you, the worker, to make such a decision for the client would generally be considered

    A. *appropriate,* because you can save time and expense by sharing your knowledge of neighborhoods with the client
    B. *inappropriate,* because workers should not help clients with this type of decision
    C. *appropriate,* because this will help the client to develop confidence in her ability to make decisions
    D. *inappropriate* because the client should be encouraged to accept the responsibility of making this decision

23._____

24. Your client, an elderly man left unable to care for himself after a stroke, has been referred for home-attendant services, but insists that he does not need these services. You believe that the man considers this to be an insult to his pride and that he will not allow himself to admit that he needs help.
    Of the following, the *MOST* appropriate action for you to take is to

    A. withdraw the referral for home-attendant services and allow the client to try to take care of himself
    B. process the request for home-attendant services on the assumption that the client will soon realize that he cannot care for himself
    C. discuss with the client your interpretation of his problem and attempt to persuade him to accept home-attendant services
    D. tell the client that he will have no further opportunity to apply for home-attendant services if he does not accept them at this time

24._____

25. A worker making a field visit to investigate a complaint of child abuse finds that the parents of the child are a racially mixed couple. The child appears poorly dressed and unruly.
    Of the following, the *MOST* appropriate approach for the worker to take in this situation is to

    A. take the child aside and ask him privately if either of his parents ever mistreats him
    B. determine if prejudice against the couple has led them to use the child as a scapegoat
    C. question the non-minority parent closely for signs of resentment of the child's mixed parentage
    D. observe the relationship between parents and child for indications of abuse by the parents

25._____

KEY (CORRECT ANSWERS)

1.	A	11.	D
2.	C	12.	A
3.	A	13.	B
4.	B	14.	B
5.	C	15.	A
6.	D	16.	B
7.	C	17.	B
8.	A	18.	B
9.	D	19.	D
10.	A	20.	C

21.	D
22.	B
23.	D
24.	C
25.	D

EXAMINATION SECTION
TEST 1

DIRECTIONS: Each question or incomplete statement is followed by several suggested answers or completions. Select the one that *BEST* answers the question or completes the statement. *PRINT THE LETTER OF THE CORRECT ANSWER IN THE SPACE AT THE RIGHT.*

1. A client tells you that he is extremely upset by the treatment that he received from Center personnel at the information desk.
Which of the following is the *BEST* way to handle this complaint during the interview?

    A. Explain to the client that he probably misinterpreted what occurred at the information desk
    B. Let the client express his feelings and then proceed with the interview
    C. Tell the client that you are not concerned with the personnel at the information desk
    D. Escort the client to the information desk to find out what really happened

1.____

2. As a worker in the foster home division, you are reviewing a case record to determine whether a 13-year-old boy, in foster care because of neglect and mistreatment by his natural parents, should be returned home. The natural parents, who want to take the child back, have been in family counseling, with encouraging results, and have improved their living conditions.
Of the following, it would be appropriate to recommend that the child

    A. remain with the foster parents, since this is a documented case of child abuse
    B. remain with the foster parents until they are ready to send him home
    C. be returned to his natural parents, since they have made positive efforts to change their behavior toward the child
    D. be returned to his natural parents, because continued separation will cause irreparable damage to the child

2.____

3. You are finishing an interview with a client in which you have explained to her the procedure she must go through to apply for income maintenance.
Of the following, the *BEST* way for you to make sure that she has fully understood the procedure is to ask her

    A. whether she feels she has understood your explanation of the procedure
    B. whether she has any questions to ask you about the procedure
    C. to describe the procedure to you in her own words
    D. a few questions to test her understanding of the procedure

3.____

4. Mrs. Carey, a widow with five children, has come to the field office to seek foster care for her 13-year-old daughter, who has often been truant from school and has recently been caught shoplifting. Mrs. Carey says that she cannot maintain a proper home environment for the other four children and deal with her daughter at the same time.
Of the following, you should *FIRST*

    A. process Mrs. Carey's request for placement of her daughter in a foster care agency
    B. interview both Mrs. Carey and her daughter to get a more complete picture of the situation
    C. suggest to Mrs. Carey that she might be able to manage if she obtained homemaker services
    D. warn the daughter that she will be sent away from home if she does not change her behavior

4.____

5. During a group orientation meeting with couples who wish to adopt babies through your agency, one couple asks you how they should deal with the question of whether the child should be told that he is adopted.
   Of the following, your *BEST* response to this couple is to

    A. tell them to conceal from the child the fact that he is adopted
    B. suggest that they lead the child to believe that his natural parents are dead
    C. tell them to inform the child that they know nothing about his natural parents
    D. explore with them their feelings about revealing to the child that he is adopted

5.____

6. You are beginning an investigation of an anonymous complaint that a welfare client has a concealed bank account. Of the following, the *FIRST* step you should generally take in conducting this investigation is to

    A. confront the client with the complaint during an office interview
    B. try to track down the source of the anonymous complaint
    C. make a surprise visit to the client in his home to question him
    D. gather any available information from bank and agency records

6.____

7. When investigating the location of an absent parent, the worker frequently interviews the parent's friends and neighbors. The worker often writes down the information given by the person interviewed and, at the end of the interview, summarizes the information to the person.
   For the worker to do this is, generally,

    A. *good practice,* because the person interviewed will be Impressed by the efficiency of the worker
    B. *poor practice,* because the person interviewed may become impatient with the worker for repeating the information
    C. *good practice,* because the person interviewed has an opportunity to correct any errors the worker may have in recording the information
    D. *poor practice,* because summarizing the information may encourage the person to waste time adding and changing information

7.____

8. During an interview for the purpose of investigating a charge of child abuse, a client first denied that she had abused her child, but then burst into tears and promised that she *will never do it again.*
   Of the following, the *MOST* appropriate action for the worker to take in this situation is to

    A. tell the client that, since she has already lied, it is difficult to believe that she will keep her promise
    B. show a concern for the client's feelings but tell her that you will have to report your findings and refer her for help
    C. determine the extent to which the child was abused and close the case if no permanent harm was done
    D. explain to the client that she has already done enough harm to the child and you must, therefore, recommend placement

8.____

9. As a worker involved in locating absent parents, you have obtained information indicating that the address for the putative father is the same as the client's address. In order to determine whether, in fact, the client and putative father are living together, of the following, it would be *MOST* appropriate to

9.____

A. visit the address and question the neighbors and superintendent about the putative father
B. visit the client to ask her why she has concealed the fact that the putative father is living with her
C. file the information in the case folder and wait for confirming information
D. close the client's case and issue a recoupment notice to the putative father

10. A client claims that she never received a welfare check that was due her. As part of your investigation of her claim, you obtain from the bank a copy of the check, which has been endorsed with her name and cashed.
Of the following, the *BEST* procedure for you to follow in this investigation is to

    10.____

A. end the investigation immediately, since the client's claim cannot be proved
B. interview the client and show her the copy of the cashed check
C. tell the client that you have evidence that her claim is false
D. say nothing about the cashed check and try to trap the client in a false statement

11. As part of the investigation to locate an absent father, you make a field visit to interview one of the father's friends. Before beginning the interview, you identify yourself to the friend and show him your official identification.
For you to do this is, generally,

    11.____

A. *good practice,* because the friend will have proof that you are authorized to make such confidential investigations
B. *poor practice,* because the friend may not answer your questions when he knows why you are interviewing him
C. *good practice,* because your supervisor can confirm from the friend that you actually made the interview
D. *poor practice,* because the friend may warn the absent father that your agency is looking for him

12. As a field office worker you are investigating a citizen's complaint charging a mother of three children with child neglect. The mother tells you that her husband has become depressed after losing his job and is often abusive to her, and that this situation has made her feel anxious and has made it difficult for her to care for the children properly.
Which one of the following is the *BEST* way for you to respond to this situation?

    12.____

A. Tell the mother that she must do everything possible to help her husband find a job
B. Arrange to meet the husband so you can explain to him the consequences of his behavior
C. Investigate the complaint, report your findings, and refer the family for counseling or other appropriate services
D. Suggest that the family obtain homemaker services so that the mother can go to work

13. You are interviewing a client in his home as part of your investigation of an anonymous complaint that he has been receiving Medicaid fraudulently. During the interview, the client frequently interrupts your questions to discuss the hardships of his life and the bitterness he feels about his medical condition.
Of the following, the *BEST* way for you to deal with these discussions is to

    13.____

A. cut them off abruptly, since the client is probably just trying to avoid answering your questions

B. listen patiently, since these discussions may be helpful to the client and may give you information for your investigation

C. remind the client that you are investigating a complaint against him and he must answer directly

D. seek to gain the client's confidence by discussing any personal or medical problems which you yourself may have

14. While interviewing an absent father to determine his ability to pay child support, you realize that his answers to some of your questions contradict his answers to other questions. Of the following, the *BEST* way for you to try to get accurate information from the father is to

14.____

A. confront him with his contradictory answers and demand an explanation from him
B. use your best judgment as to which of his answers are accurate and question him accordingly
C. tell him that he has misunderstood your questions and that he must clarify his answers
D. ask him the same questions in different words and follow up his answers with related questions

15. You are assigned to investigate a complaint of child neglect made against a minority mother by her non-minority neighbor. During an interview with you, the neighbor states that the mother allows her children to run around the streets half-dressed till late at night, and adds: *Of course, what can you expect from any of those people anyway?* Of the following, your *MOST* appropriate action is to

15.____

A. end the investigation, since the neighbor is clearly too prejudiced to be reliable
B. tell the mother that the neighbor has made a complaint of child neglect against her
C. seek evidence to support the complaint of child neglect made by the neighbor
D. continue the interview with the neighbor in an attempt to get at the root of his prejudice against the mother

16. You are interviewing a couple with regard to available services for the husband's aged mother. During the interview, the husband casually mentions that he and his wife are thinking about becoming foster parents and would like to get some information on foster care programs offered through the department of social services. Of the following agencies within social services, the *MOST* appropriate one for you to refer this couple to is

16.____

A. family and adult services
B. special services for children
C. bureau of child support
D. special services for adults

17. You have been helping one of your clients to obtain medical assistance for her two young children. Accidentally, you obtain evidence that the client may be involved in a criminal scheme to collect duplicate welfare checks at several different addresses. Of the following offices of the department of social services, the *MOST* appropriate one to which you should report this evidence is

17.____

A. the inspector general
B. case intake and management
C. the general counsel
D. income support

Questions 18-25.

DIRECTIONS: Questions 18 through 25 are to be answered *SOLELY* on the basis of the FACT SITUATION and REPORT FORM.

FACT SITUATION

On June 5, 2013, Mary Adams (Case No. ADC-2095732), lining at 1507 Montague Street, Apt. 3C, Brooklyn, New York, applied and was accepted for public assistance for herself and her three dependant children. Her husband, John, had left their home after an argument the previous week and had not returned, leaving Mrs. Adams without funds of any kind. She had tried to contact him at his place of employment, but was told that he had resigned several days prior to her call. When the Case Worker questioned Mrs. Adams about her husband's employment, income, and bank accounts, Mrs. Adams stated that he had done carpentry work during most of the years he had worked; his last known employer had been the Avco Lumber Company, 309 Amber Street, Queens, New York, where he had earned a weekly salary of $300. She then showed the Case Worker two bankbooks in her husband's name, which indicated a balance of $500 in one account and $275 in the other. A visit to Mr. Brown, a neighbor of the Adams', by the Case Worker, revealed that Mr. Adams had also told Mr. Brown about the existence of the bankbooks. A visit to the Avco Lumber Company by the Case Worker confirmed that Mr. Adams' gross salary had been $300 a week. This visit also revealed that Mr. Adams was a member of the Woodworkers' Union, Local #7, and that Mr. Adams' previous home address for the period from February '02 to June '08 was 1109 Wellington Street, Brooklyn, New York.

REPORT FORM

A. **CLIENT**:

   1. Name:_____

   2. Address: _____

   3. Case No.: _____

   4. Acceptance Date:_____

   5. No. of Dependent Children: _____

B. **ABSENT PARENT**:

   1. Name:_____

   2. Date of birth _____

   3. Place of Birth:_____

   4. Present Address: _____

   5. Regular Occupation: _____

   6. Union Affiliation: _____

   7. Name of Last Employer:_____

   8. Address of Last Employer: _____

   9.   a.   Weekly Earnings (Gross):_____

        b.   How Verified:_____

   10. a.   Weekly Earnings (Net):   _____

        b.   How Verified:_____

   11. a.   Amount of Bank Accounts:_____

        b.   How Verified:_____

   12. Social Security No.:_____

   13. Last Known Home Address: _____

   14. Previous Addresses:_____

18. Based on the information given in the FACT SITUATION, the *MOST* appropriate of the   18.____
following entries for item B.II.b is:

    A. *Revealed to Case Worker by Mrs. Adams*
    B. *Confirmed by visit to Mr. Brown*
    C. *Revealed by Woodworkers' Union, Local #7*
    D. *Confirmed by bankbooks shown by Mrs. Adams*

19. The *one* of the following which *BEST* answers item B.4 is: 19.____

    A. *unknown*
    B. *c/o Avco Lumber Company*
    C. *1109 Wellington Street, Brooklyn, New York*
    D. *1507 Montague Street, Brooklyn, New York*

20. Based on the information given in the FACT SITUATION, it is *NOT* possible to answer   20.____
item

    A. A.2   B. A.5   C. B.6   D. B.10

21. The *one* of the following which would be *LEAST* helpful in tracing the missing parent is   21.____
information found in item

    A. B.12   B. B.10.a   C. B.6   D. B.1

22. Based on the information given in the FACT SITUATION, it is *most likely* that the *SAME*   22.____
entry would be made for items

    A. A.1 and B.1   B. A.4 and B.2
    C. B.9.a and B.10.a   D. A.2 and B.13

23. Based on the information in the FACT SITUATION, the entry : *1109 Wellington Street,*   23.____
Brooklyn, New York would *most likely* be placed for item

    A. A.2   B. B.4   C. B.8   D. B.14

24. The *one* of the following items that can be answered based on the information given in   24.____
the FACT SITUATION is

    A. B.2   B. B.3   C. B.9.b   D. B.12

25. Based on the information given in the FACT SITUATION, the figure *775* would appear in   25.____
the entry for

    A. A.3   B. B.12   C. B.9.a   D. B.11.a

———————

KEY (CORRECT ANSWERS)

1.	B		11.	A
2.	C		12.	C
3.	C		13.	B
4.	B		14.	D
5.	D		15.	C
6.	D		16.	B
7.	C		17.	A
8.	B		18.	D
9.	A		19.	A
10.	B		20.	D

21.	B
22.	D
23.	D
24.	C
25.	D

———

TEST 2

DIRECTIONS: Each question or incomplete statement is followed by several suggested answers or completions. Select the one that BEST answers the question or completes the statement. *PRINT THE LETTER OF THE CORRECT ANSWER IN THE SPACE AT THE RIGHT.*

1. A worker in a senior adult center is approached by one of his clients, an elderly man living alone and suffering from severe arthritis, who asks him how to go about obtaining homemaker services through the department of social services.
   Of the following, the *MOST* appropriate office of the department to which the worker should refer this client is:

   A. income support
   B. protective services for adults
   C. income maintenance
   D. case intake and management

   1.____

2. Workers assigned to locate absent parents frequently ask various governmental agencies to search their records for information useful in determining the address of the person they are seeking.
   Of the following, the agency which is likely to be useful *most frequently* for this purpose is the

   A. motor vehicle bureau
   B. office of the district attorney
   C. department of investigation
   D. health and hospitals corporation

   2.____

Questions 3-7.

DIRECTIONS: Questions 3 through 7 are to be answered *SOLELY* on the basis of the FACT SITUATION and PRELIMINARY INVESTIGATION FORM.

FACT SITUATION

COMPLAINT:

On March 1, Mrs. Mona Willard, a neighbor of the Smith family, reported to the Police Department that the Smith children, were being severely neglected, and she requested that an investigation be conducted. She based her complaint on the fact that, since the time three weeks ago when Janet Smith's husband, Charles, deserted Mrs. Smith and their two children, John, age 2, and Darlene, age 4, the children have been seen wandering in the neighborhood at all hours, inadequately dressed against the cold.

INVESTIGATION:

Investigation by the Police Department and the Department of Social Services revealed that the above charge was true and, further, that Mrs. Smith had inflicted cruel and harsh physical treatment upon the children in an attempt to discipline them. The children were immediately removed from their parent's care and placed in a medical facility for tests and observation. It as found that the children were suffering from serious malnutrition and anemia and that they also showed signs of emotional disturbance.

CASE ACTION DECISION:

Conferences which you, the Case Worker, have held with Dr. Charles Jordan, a physician treating Mrs. Smith, and with Ellen Farraday, a psychiatric social worker from the Mental Health Consultation Center, confirm that Mrs. Smith is emotionally unstable at the present time and cannot care for her children. A written report from the Chief Resident Physician at the hospital where the children have been placed indicates that both children are presently doing well, but when released will need the security of an emotionally stable atmosphere. It has therefore been decided that placement in a foster he ia necessary for the children until such time as Mrs. Smith is judged to be capable of caring for them.

PRELIMINARY INVESTIGATION FORM			
1. Child(ren) in Need of Protection :			
a. Name(s): _____			
b. Age (s) : _____			
2. Alleged Perpetrator :			
a. Name: _____			
b. Relationship: _____			
3. Present Status of Child(ren):			
☐ a. Remaining with Subject Pending Investigation			
☐ b. Removed to Relatives			
☐ c. Removed to Foster Care			
☐ d. In Hospital			
☐ e. Other			
4. Actions or Services Needed for Child(ren):			
☐ a. Housekeeper			
☐ b. Homemaker			
☐ c. Day Care			
☐ d. Home Attendant			
☐ e. Relatives			
☐ f. Foster Care			
5. Contacts Made to Support Case Action Decision:	I Phone	II Personal	III Written
a. Medical; School	☐	☐	☐
b. Relatives	☐	☐	☐
c. Social Agency	☐	☐	☐
d. Other	☐	☐	☐

3. The *one* of the following that should be entered in space 2.b is   3.____

    A. mother   B. father   C. neighbor   D. physician

4. The *one* of the following boxes that should be checked in item 3 is   4.____

    A. a   B. c   C. d   D. e

5. The *one* of the following boxes that should be checked in item 4 is   5.____

    A. a   B. c   C. d   D. f

6. Based on the information given in the FACT SITUATION, the boxes that should be   6.____
checked off in item 5 are:

    A. a-II, a-III, c-II   B. a-II, c-II, c-III
    C. a-I, a-II, a-III   D. b-II, c-I, c-II

7. The *one* of the following that would *CORRECTLY* appear as part of the entry to item 1.a   7.____
is

    A. Mona   B. Janet   C. Darlene   D. Ellen

Questions 8-12.

DIRECTIONS: Answer Questions 8 through 12 *SOLELY* on the basis of the information contained in the following passage:

It is desirable, whenever possible, to have long-term elderly patients return to their own homes after hospitalization, provided that the medical condition is not acute. Of course, there must be room for the patient; the family must be able to provide some necessary care; and a physician's services must be available. Although the patient's family may be able to provide most services for the patient in his own home, this is generally unlikely because of the nature of the illness and the patient's need for a variety of services. Recently, hospital personnel, public health workers, visiting nurse associations, and community leaders have been developing home-care programs, which make the services of the hospital available to the patient who is not ill enough to require the concentrated technical facilities of a general hospital, but who is unable to attend an outpatient clinic or a physician's office. These services are those of the physician, visiting nurse, physical therapist, occupational therapist, social worker, and homemaker, as needed. There is also provision for readmission to the hospital for specific purposes and return to home care.

8. According to the passage above, it would be *UNDESIRABLE* to have an elderly patient   8.____
return to his own home after hospitalization when the patient

    A. requires the services of a doctor
    B. may be in immediate danger due to his medical condition
    C. is under physical or occupational therapy
    D. cannot go to the outpatient clinic of the hospital

9. According to the passage above, the *services of the hospital* which are made available   9.____
by home-care programs include those of

    A. dietitians   B. visiting nurses
    C. public health administrators   D. community workers

10. The *one* of the following statements about home-care programs which is *BEST* supported by the paragraph above is that home-care programs   10.____

    A. have been developed in part by hospital personnel
    B. relieve workloads of hospital personnel
    C. decrease public expenditures for hospitalization of the elderly
    D. reduce readmissions of elderly patients to hospitals

11. According to the above passage, home-care programs would be *LEAST* likely to include the services of a   11.____

    A. homemaker   B. social worker
    C. physician   D. hospital technician

12. It may be *inferred* from the passage above that a *MAJOR* purpose of home-care programs is to   12.____

    A. increase the demand for physicians, nurses, and other medical personnel
    B. provide patients in their homes with services similar to those provided in hospitals
    C. reduce the need for general hospitals and outpatient clinics
    D. relieve the family of their responsibility of caring for the patient

Questions 13-17.

DIRECTIONS: Answer Questions 13 through 17 *SOLELY* on the basis of the information contained in the following DUTIES STATEMENT.

DUTIES STATEMENT OF THE VIOLATION CENTER (VC) CASE WORKER

1. Receives telephone, mail, and in-person reports of suspected violations from mandated and non-mandated sources, as well as from the New York State Violation Bureau (NYSVB). Informs mandated sources that they must send a written summary of their report, on form DSS-555, within 48 hours, to the Central Office of VC, 265 Church Street, New York, N. Y.

2. Completes in-office portion of DSS-555 received from mandated sources as fully as possible. Checks that report summary is specific, factual, and detailed. (See NYSVB Instructions on page 213.)

3. When DSS-555 is received, clears Central Office of VC for any previous record of violation on file in Central Office. If record exists, enters additional information from file record on to DSS-555. Also requests Central Office Clerk to provide appropriate record number of previous record and enters additional information from file record on to DSS-555. Also requests Central Office Clerk to provide appropriate record number of previous record and enters it in correct box on form.

4. Determines appropriate Central Office Sex Code and Reporting Source Code for each violation. (The Codes are in the VC Manual.) The codes are then entered on the bottom of the reverse side of the DSS-555.

5. Determines appropriate Service Area Code for the address in the summary. The address is the location of the violation, if known. (If the location of the violation is unknown, the address of the primary witness shall be used.) Enters Service Area Code on reverse of DSS-555. All report summaries involving violations by N.Y.C. employees are sent to the Manhattan Borough Office of VC for clearance and transmittal to BEM.

---

13. According to the DUTIES STATEMENT above, when a report of a suspected violation is received, a written summary of their report on DSS-555 must be sent within 48 hours by   13.____

   A.   mandated sources   B.   non-mandated sources C.   the NYSVB
   D.   mandated and non-mandated sources, as well as by the NYSVB

14. From the above DUTIES STATEMENT, it may be *inferred* that the Case Worker whose duties are described is *most likely* assigned to   14.____

   A.   the Manhattan Borough Office of VC
   B.   the New York State Violation Bureau
   C.   the Central Office of VC
   D.   BEM

15. According to the DUTIES STATEMENT above, the Central Office Sex Code is entered on the DSS-555   15.____

   A.   on the opposite side from the Service Area Code
   B.   on the front of the form
   C.   above the Service Area Code on the form
   D.   on the bottom of the back of the form

16. According to the above DUTIES STATEMENT, a Case Worker can determine the appropriate Reporting Source Code for a violation by consulting   16.____

   A.   NYSVB Instructions   B.   the Central Office Clerk
   C.   the VC Manual   D.   the Service Area Code

17. As used in paragraph 2 of the DUTIES STATEMENT above, the word *detailed* means, most nearly,   17.____

   A.   fully descriptive   B.   complicated
   C.   of considerable length   D.   well-written

Questions 18-25.

DIRECTIONS: Refer to the following SEMI-MONTHLY FAMILY ALLOWANCE SCHEDULE and CONVERSION TABLE when answering Questions 18 through 25.

FIGURE NO. 1

SEMI-MONTHLY FAMILY ALLOWANCE SCHEDULE FOR MAINTENANCE OF LEGALLY RESPONSIBLE RELATIVE AND DEPENDENTS, BASED UPON
TOTAL NUMBER OF PERSONS IN PRESENT HOUSEHOLD. (ALL SURPLUS IS TO BE USED AS CONTRIBUTION TO RECIPIENTS OF PUBLIC ASSISTANCE.)

TOTAL NUMBER OF PERSONS IN PRESENT HOUSEHOLD	ONE	TWO	THREE	FOUR	FIVE	SIX	EACH ADDITIONAL PERSON
SEMI-MONTHLY FAMILY ALLOWANCE	$1600	$1915	$2200	$2605	$2800	$3205	$350

FIGURE NO. 2

CONVERSION TABLE - WEEKLY TO SEMI-MONTHLY AMOUNTS

DOLLARS				CENTS			
Weekly Amount	Semi-Monthly Amount	Weekly Amount	Semi-Monthly Amount	Weekly Amount	Semi-Monthly Amount	Weekly Amount	Semi-Monthly Amount
$10.00	$ 21.70	$510.00	$1105.00	$0.10	$0.20	$5.10	$11.10
20.00	43.30	520.00	1126.70	0.20	0.40	5.20	11.30
30.00	65.00	530.00	1148.30	0.30	0.70	5.30	11.50
40.00	86.70	540.00	1170.00	0.40	0.90	5.40	11.70
50.00	108.30	550.00	1191.70	0.50	1.10	5.50	11.90
60.00	130.00	560.00	1213.30	0.60	1.30	5.60	12.10
70.00	151.70	570.00	1235.00	0.70	1.50	5.70	12.40
80.00	173.30	580.00	1256.70	0.80	1.70	5.80	12.60
90.00	195.00	590.00	1278.30	0.90	2.00	5.90	12.80
100.00	216.70	600.00	1300.00	1.00	2.20	6.00	13.00
110.00	238.30	610.00	1321.70	1.10	2.40	6.10	13.20
120.00	260.00	620.00	1343.30	1.20	2.60	6.20	13.40
130.00	281.70	630.00	1365.00	1.30	2.80	6.30	13.70
140.00	303.30	640.00	1386.70	1.40	3.00	6.40	13.90
150.00	325.00	650.00	1408.30	1.50	3.30	6.50	14.10
160.00	346.70	660.00	1430.00	1.60	3.50	6.60	14.30
170.00	368.30	670.00	1451.70	1.70	3.70	6.70	14.50
180.00	390.00	680.00	1473.30	1.80	3.90	6.80	14.70
190.00	411.70	690.00	1495.00	1.90	4.10	6.90	15.00
200.00	433.30	700.00	1516.70	2.00	4.30	7.00	15.20
210.00	455.00	710.00	1538.30	2.10	4.60	7.10	15.40
220.00	476.70	720.00	1560.00	2.20	4.80	7.20	15.60
230.00	498.30	730.00	1581.70	2.30	5.00	7.30	15.80
240.00	520.00	740.00	1603.30	2.40	5.20	7.40	16.00
250.00	541.70	750.00	1625.00	2.50	5.40	7.50	16.30
260.00	563.30	760.00	1646.70	2.60	5.60	7.60	16.50
270.00	585.00	770.00	1668.30	2.70	5.90	7.70	16.70
280.00	606.70	780.00	1690.00	2.80	6.10	7.80	16.90
290.00	628.30	790.00	1711.70	2.90	6.30	7.90	17.10
300.00	650.00	800.00	1733.30	3.00	6.50	8.00	17.30
310.00	671.70	810.00	1755.00	3.10	6.70	8.10	17.60
320.00	693.30	820.00	1776.70	3.20	6.90	8.20	17.80
330.00	715.00	830.00	1798.30	3.30	7.20	8.30	18.00
340.00	736.70	840.00	1820.00	3.40	7.40	8.40	18.20
350.00	783.00	850.00	1841.70	3.50	7.60	8.50	18.40
360.00	780.00	860.00	1863.30	3.60	7.80	8.60	18.60
370.00	801.70	870.00	1885.00	3.70	8.00	8.70	18.90
380.00	823.30	880.00	1906.70	3.80	8.20	8.80	19.10
390.00	845.00	890.00	1928.30	3.90	8.50	8.90	18.30
400.00	866.70	900.00	1950.00	4.00	8.70	9.00	19.50
410.00	888.30	910.00	1971.70	4.10	8.90	9.10	19.70
420.00	910.00	920.00	1993.30	4.20	9.10	9.20	19.90
430.00	931.70	930.00	2015.00	4.30	9.30	9.30	20.20
440.00	953.30	940.00	2036.70	4.40	9.50	9.40	20.40
450.00	975.00	950.00	2058.30	4.50	9.80	9.50	20.60
460.00	996.70	960.00	2080.00	4.60	10.00	9.60	20.80
470.00	1018.30	970.00	2101.70	4.70	10.20	9.70	21.00
480.00	1040.00	980.00	2123.30	4.80	10.40	9.80	21.20
490.00	1061.70	990.00	2145.00	4.90	10.60	9.90	21.50
500.00	1083.30	1000.00	2166.70	5.00	10.80		

DIRECTIONS: Questions 18 through 25 are to be answered *SOLELY* on the basis of the SEMI-MONTHLY FAMILY ALLOWANCE SCHEDULE FOR MAINTENANCE OF LEGALLY RESPONSIBLE RELATIVE (FIGURE NO. 1) and CONVERSION TABLE (FIGURE NO. 2) given on pages 5 and 6 and the information and case situations given below.

Questions 18 through 21 are based on Case Situation No. 1;
Questions 22 through 25 are based on Case Situation No. 2.

INFORMATION

Legally responsible relatives living apart from persons on public assistance are asked to contribute toward the support of these persons. The amount of contribution depends on several factors, such as the number of persons in the legally responsible relative's present household who are dependent on his income (including himself), the amount of his gross income, and his expenses incident to employment. Since his contribution is computed on a semi-monthly basis, all figures must be broken down into semi-monthly amounts. Weekly amounts can be converted into semi-monthly amounts by using the conversion table on page 6.

The amount of support is computed as follows:

1. Determine total weekly gross income (the wages or salary *before* payroll deductions) of legally responsible relative.
2. Deduct all weekly expenses incident to employment such as federal, state, and city income taxes, Social Security payments, State Disability Insurance payments, union dues, cost of transportation, and $10.00 maximum per work day for lunch.
3. Remaining income shall be considered as weekly net income of legally responsible relative.
4. Convert weekly net income to semi-monthly net income, using data in FIGURE NO. 2.
5. Semi-monthly net income is compared to the semi-monthly allowance (see FIGURE NO. 1). If there is an excess of net income, then that amount is considered available as the contribution to the public assistance household. If the semi-monthly allowance is greater than the semi-monthly net income, then there is an income deficit, and there is no income available as a contribution to the public assistance household.
6. The formula for computing the semi-monthly contribution is:

> Semi-Monthly Net Income
> - <u>Semi-Monthly Family Allowance</u>
> = Semi-Monthly Amount of Income Available Towards Contribution to Public Assistance Household

Case Situation No. 1

Mr. Andrew Young is separated from his wife and family and lives with one dependent in a 3-room furnished apartment. Mr. Young is employed as a dishwasher and his gross wages are $1000.00 per week. He is employed 5 days a week and spends $14.00 a day carfare. He spends $20.00 a work day on lunch. His weekly salary deductions are as follows:

Federal Income Tax	$142.30
State Income Tax	26.00
City Income Tax	9.80
Social Security	62.10
New York State Disability Insurance	5.30
Union Dues	5.00

Mr. Young's wife and two children, for whom he is legally responsible, are currently receiving public assistance.

Case Situation No. 2
    Mr. Donald Wilson resides with six dependents in a seven-room unfurnished apartment. Mr. Wilson is employed as an automobile salesman and his gross wages are $4000.00 per week. He is employed five days a week and spends $10.00 a day carfare. He spends $50.00 a work day for lunch. His weekly salary deductions are as follows:

Federal Income Tax	$705.50
State Income Tax	150.00
City Income Tax	97.00
Social Security	301.00
New York State Disability Insurance	52.50
Union Dues	Not Union Member

    Mr. Wilson is the only wage earner in his present household. His legal wife and minor child, for whom he is legally responsible, are both receiving public assistance.

NOTE: When answering Questions 18 through 21, refer to Case Situation No. 1.

18.   The *weekly amount* that Mr. Young contributes toward Social Security, New York State Disability Insurance, Income Taxes, and Union Dues is, most nearly,   18._____

    A. $214.70   B. $250.50   C. $320.50   D. $370.50

19.   The *total amount* of all weekly expenses incident to Mr. Young's employment which should be deducted from his weekly gross earnings, is, most nearly,   19._____

    A. $214.70   B. $250.50   C. $370.50   D. $420.50

20.   *Which one* of the following amounts is Mr. Young's *semimonthly net income?*   20._____

    A. $1259.00   B. $1363.90   C. $1623.90   D. $1701.50

21.   The *semi-monthly amount* of income available to the contribution to Mr. Young's wife and two children is, most nearly,   21._____

    A. $0.00   B. $23.90   C. $236.10   D. $551.10

NOTE: When answering Questions 22 through 25, refer to Case Situation No. 2.

22.   The *weekly amount* that Mr. Wilson contributes toward Social Security, New York State Disability Insurance, Federal Income Tax, and Union Dues is, most nearly,   22._____

    A. $1059.00   B. $1159.00   C. $1306.00   D. $1406.00

23.   The *total amount* of all weekly expenses incident to Mr. Wilson's employment, which should be deducted from his weekly gross earnings, is, most nearly,   23._____

    A. $1159.00   B. $1306.00   C. $1406.00   D. $1606.00

24.   The *semi-monthly family allowance* for Mr. Wilson and his six dependents is, most nearly,   24._____

    A. $2594.00   B. $3205.00   C. $3555.00   D. $4000.00

25.   The *semi-monthly amount* of Mr. Wilson's income available for contribution to his wife and child is, most nearly,   25._____

    A. $1633.00   B. $2065.40   C. $2594.00   D. $2810.20

KEY (CORRECT ANSWERS)

1.	D		11.	D
2.	A		12.	B
3.	A		13.	A
4.	C		14.	C
5.	D		15.	D
6.	A		16.	C
7.	C		17.	A
8.	B		18.	B
9.	B		19.	C
10.	A		20.	B

21.	A
22.	A
23.	C
24.	C
25.	B

———

EXAMINATION SECTION
TEST 1

DIRECTIONS : Each question or incomplete statement is followed by several suggested answers or completions. Select the one that BEST answers the question or completes the statement. *PRINT THE LETTER OF THE CORRECT ANSWER IN THE SPACE AT THE RIGHT.*

1. One day an elderly man asks you if he can apply for Social Security at the welfare office. Your response should be to   1.____

   A. tell him that it is foolish to think he can apply for Social Security at the welfare office
   B. take him back to his apartment because he is too old to be roaming the streets asking questions
   C. explain that Social Security is a federal program and direct him to the nearest Social Security office
   D. call his daughter and tell her that the family should take better care of their father

2. One of your duties is to occasionally visit clients. On one occasion, you visit Mrs. B., who needs assistance in referral of her children for day care so that she may enter a job training program. She has postponed completing the referral.
   What should you do in this situation?   2.____

   A. Tell her that if she doesn't hurry there will be no room at the day care center and the training program will be closed.
   B. Make the arrangements and tell Mrs. B. that she should do what you say.
   C. Remember that all people who ask for help are not always ready to receive it and continue to allow Mrs. B. time to complete the referral by herself.
   D. The next time Mrs. B. asks for help, see that she gets it as slowly as possible.

3. Assume that you are trying to contact a community group to offer to meet with their representative to explain a new agency policy about intake procedures.
   In order to "get your message across," you should   3.____

   A. write a short concise letter explaining why you want to meet with them and when you will be available
   B. write a short letter stating only that it is important that they contact you in order to arrange a meeting
   C. ask a secretary to help you because you do not really like to write to groups
   D. call the agency rather than write since you know someone there

4. It is necessary for you to call the director of a head start center in order to discuss a training program for teaching aides. The operator asks who you are and what you wish to discuss with the director.
   Your response should be to   4.____

   A. tell her that you would rather explain to the director and you want to speak to her immediately
   B. identify yourself, your department and the nature of your business with the director
   C. hang up and try to call again when another operator is on duty
   D. tell your supervisor that the operator at the head start center is rude and you would rather not be asked to call there again

5. Mrs. A. wants her children to go to summer camp. She has received the request forms, but does not understand all of the questions and you are asked to help her complete them. She comes to the office at the appointed time.
   Of the following, the action you should take is to

   A. tell her she has taken so long that maybe the children will not go to camp
   B. see her as quickly as possible, explain the questions to her and help her in completing the forms
   C. help her, but tell her she will have to learn to read better and refer her to an evening school
   D. fill out the forms for her by yourself

   5.____

6. Mrs. B. needs a referral to the cancer clinic. You contact the clinic and make arrangements for her visit. You go to her home to inform her about the time because she has no phone. She thanks you for your help and then offers you a piece of jewelry that appears to be rather expensive. Of the following, the action you should take is to

   A. take the gift because you don't want to hurt her feelings
   B. tell her that she is foolish and should spend her money on herself
   C. explain to her that you are pleased with her thoughtfulness, but you are unable to accept the gift
   D. refuse the gift and get someone else to make referrals in the future because she is trying to pay you for your help

   6.____

7. Mrs. C., a seemingly healthy, intelligent woman whose husband is disabled, and who works part time, asks for help in getting homemaker services.
   Of the following, the action you should take is to

   A. give Mrs. C. the necessary information and help her get the services
   B. tell Mrs. C. that you do not feel she needs these services since her husband is capable of helping
   C. make note of her request since you do not feel it is urgent
   D. refer her to a caseworker since she obviously needs help in defining her role as a woman

   7.____

8. When you are interviewing clients, it is important to notice and record how they say what they say - angrily, nervously, or with "body English" - because these signs may

   A. tell you that the client's words are the opposite of what the client feels and you may need to dig to find out what those feelings are
   B. be the prelude to violent behavior which no aide is prepared to handle
   C. show that the client does not really deserve serious consideration
   D. be important later should you be asked to defend what you did for the client

   8.____

9. You are recording a visit you have made with a client who was angry and abusive to you during the interview. At one point you lost your temper and said some things that you immediately regretted. You are embarrassed to record that you lost your temper. However, it would be desirable to record this MAINLY because

   A. you would feel guilty if you did not record it
   B. your supervisor might hear about it from the client, so it would be better to have it written down from your point of view
   C. your supervisor can use the information to help you to improve your skills
   D. it is agency policy to write down everything

   9.____

10. Through one of your clients you learn that a day care program's hours have been extended. You confirm this information with the day care center.
It is then MOST important for you to

    A. make a note of this fact, since it will mean you have to change your schedule in working with the client
    B. add this information to your personal resource file so that you can refer other clients to the day care program
    C. inform your supervisor of the new information so that it can be added to the central resource file
    D. ignore the information, since your client does not need to have her child in day care for any extra hours

10.____

11. You are sent to a meeting of day-care parents to explain the programs of your agency. One of the parents becomes very angry, saying that welfare departments treat people like animals.
You should remain as calm as possible and say to the parent that

    A. he is right, but you have no control over what your agency does
    B. he is disrupting the meeting and you have come to explain a program, not to listen to complaints
    C. you understand his feelings and that sometimes clients do not get the services they wish as quickly as possible; however, you will do whatever you can to assist him
    D. he should call your supervisor tomorrow and make an appointment to discuss his feelings

11.____

12. Assume that you receive a telephone call from a very angry father. His daughter took money from his wallet, and he wants the caseworker to control the daughter. He yells, screams and swears at you.
What is the BEST way for you to respond?

    A. Hang up because you are not responsible for his daughter's actions. He shouldn't scream and swear at you.
    B. Remember to be courteous and polite at all times, never losing your temper despite the circumstances. Listen to him and assure him that the caseworker will receive his message.
    C. Transfer the call to the supervisor because you are concerned about the father's unreasonableness and do not want the responsibility of dealing with him.
    D. Tell him that behavior such as he is demonstrating is the reason his daughter steals from him.

12.____

13. Mrs. D.'s son, aged 12, has been getting into difficulty in the neighborhood. At a community meeting, she asks your help in finding worthwhile activities for him.
It is *appropriate* for you to respond to her because

    A. you should have knowledge of the social services available in the neighborhood and the activities they offer
    B. you have known Mrs. D. and her family for several years and know how much trouble she has had with her son
    C. it is your job to do what the caseworker assigns to you without question
    D. you are concerned about impressing Mrs. D. with your knowledge

13.____

14. Several clients live in your neighborhood. They know that you work for the human resources administration. One day one of them tells you that there is a rumor that another client is pregnant and asks if this is true. You know from a past discussion with the caseworker that this client is pregnant.
The BEST answer for you to give would be to

    14.____

    A.   tell her it is none of her business and if she wants to know, she should ask the caseworker
    B.   ask her who told her that this client is pregnant
    C.   explain that anything told to the agency is held in confidence and will not be shared with anyone else
    D.   tell her you don't know, but will ask when you get back to the office and let her know later

15. The area senior-citizens group asks for an agency representative to discuss old-age assistance and new SSI regulations. Your supervisor asks you to attend this meeting; however, you do not wish to go because you really do not feel that you work well with older people. In fact, you don't like them very much.
What should be your response?

    15.____

    A.   Tell the supervisor that you cannot go because you have an appointment with the doctor that day
    B.   Get another worker to go for you and assume his task while he is gone
    C.   Explain to your supervisor what problems you have in working with old-age clients
    D.   Go, because you should do the tasks that are assigned to you according to your job description

16. At a center where you are distributing literature about agency programs, a citizen comes up to you and begins to complain loudly about agency programs.
What should be your response?

    16.____

    A.   Call the police and have the complainer removed from the center
    B.   Tell him that you do not make policy; suggest that he go to the office and complain
    C.   Remain as calm as possible and ask that he discuss the complaints with you calmly. If necessary, make an appointment with him
    D.   Yell at him since this seems to be the way he relates to agency people

17. A community group is having a training program. You are sent to explain agency policy and answer questions. Providing this type of contact between the agency and community groups is *proper* because

    17.____

    A.   you like people and are a good public speaker
    B.   it is the responsibility of the agency to cooperate with community groups in order to help the public to be well informed about agency policy
    C.   you were once in the same training program and understand the kind of people who are being trained
    D.   once in a while everyone should have the opportunity to speak to a community group

18. While you are assisting in the intake area, a young man who is applying is cooperative   18._____
but begins to ask you personal questions: your age, where you live, whether you have
children and other similar questions.
You are disturbed by these questions, so you should

    A. tell him that agency policy does not allow you to answer personal questions and
       send him to another intake worker
    B. tell him it is your responsibility to ask questions, not his
    C. tell your supervisor that you do not want to work in intake because clients can get
       too nosy and you get nervous
    D. avoid answering personal questions and try to get him to return to the purpose of
       the interview

19. You are assigned to the reception area for the day. A mother arrives in the office with   19._____
three small children. In a rage, she says that she does not have enough money to feed
the children and demands that you find a home for them.
The BEST action for you to take should be to

    A. call a security officer and have him remove her and the children from the office
    B. attempt to calm her down by listening to her, attend to the children's needs and call
       for a supervisor
    C. take the children from her and ask her to leave at once
    D. call the supervisor and security because it is their job to take care of abusive cli-
       ents

20. Assume that you are interviewing a young unwed mother who has recently arrived in the   20._____
city from Alabama. She is a likable girl and is very cooperative. However, it is difficult to
understand the meaning of her conversation, due to her accent and different use of
words.
You would like to establish a good relationship with her, so you should FIRST

    A. suggest that she go to evening school so that she can learn to speak like other
       people in the city
    B. tell her that you don't understand her sometimes and you would appreciate it if she
       would explain what she means
    C. take another worker with you on visits to help you in the interview
    D. try to find a worker in the agency who has a similar background and have the case
       handled by the worker

21. A man being interviewed is entitled to Medicaid, but he refuses to sign up for it because   21._____
he says he cannot accept any form of welfare. Of the following, the BEST course of
action for an aide to take FIRST is to

    A. try to discover the reason for his feeling this way
    B. tell him that he should be glad financial help is available
    C. explain that others cannot help him if he will not help himself
    D. suggest that he speak to someone who is already on Medicaid

22. Of the following, the outcome of an interview by an aide depends MOST heavily on the   22._____

    A. personality of the interviewee
    B. personality of the aide

C.   subject matter of the questions asked
D.   interaction between aide and interviewee

23.   Some patients being interviewed are primarily interested in making a favorable impres-   23.____
       sion. The aide should be aware of the fact that such patients are more likely than other
       patients to

A.   try to anticipate the answers the interviewer is looking for
B.   answer all questions openly and frankly
C.   try to assume the role of interviewer
D.   be anxious to get the interview over as quickly as possible

24.   The type of interview which an aide usually conducts is substantially different from most   24.____
       interviewing situations in all of the following aspects EXCEPT the

A.   setting   B.   kinds of clients
C.   techniques employed   D.   kinds of problems

25.   During an interview, an aide uses a "leading question." This type of question is so-called   25.____
       because it generally

A.   starts a series of questions about one topic
B.   suggests the answer which the aide wants
C.   forms the basis for a following "trick" question
D.   sets, at the beginning, the tone of the interview

KEY(CORRECT ANSWERS)

1.	C		11.	C
2.	C		12.	B
3.	A		13.	A
4.	B		14.	C
5.	B		15.	C
6.	C		16.	C
7.	A		17.	B
8.	A		18.	D
9.	C		19.	B
10.	C		20.	B

21.	A
22.	D
23.	A
24.	C
25.	B

TEST 2

DIRECTIONS : Each question or incomplete statement is followed by several suggested answers or completions. Select the one that BEST answers the question or completes the statement. *PRINT THE LETTER OF THE CORRECT ANSWER IN THE SPACE AT THE RIGHT.*

1. Miss Lally is an old-age assistance recipient. Her health is not good and it is important that she have three good meals each day. She follows these instructions except on Friday she refuses to eat meat because of her religious beliefs. She will not even substitute fish.
   You are very concerned about this, so you should

   A. tell your supervisor so that she will go to see Miss Lally and make her eat nourishing meals on Friday
   B. call her doctor and tell him so that he will see her and explain to her that fasting is not good for her health
   C. attempt to understand her value system and accept that it is possible that she is acting in good faith with her own values even though they may be harmful to her health
   D. explain to her how important it is that she eat meat each day in order to be in good health and enjoy the remaining years of her life

1.____

2. Theodore is a junkie. Every cent he can get his hands on legally or illegally is used to supply his habit. You are angry because the junkie is destroying himself and his family. You feel that the courts should punish him for his illegal acts.
   Of the following, the BEST action for you to take is to

   A. suggest to your supervisor that the income maintenance center reduce the family grant, taking out his portion
   B. help his wife to find another apartment for her and the children away from him
   C. call the local police to find out why they are doing nothing about this man's activities in the community
   D. reconsider your ideas about punishment, remembering that punishment *alone* will not help the man to change his behavior

2.____

3. You are regularly assigned to taking Sarah Jones and her young son to the clinic. She is a very warm, friendly woman and your relationship with her is good. However, she invited you to come for dinner on Sunday and to go to a school play with her. You would like to accept the invitations because you need weekend activities and you like her. What should be your PRIMARY consideration in coming to a decision?

   A. You need friends just as she does, so you should accept the invitations
   B. You are a worker and should not be seen with a client in public places
   C. Decide whether accepting the invitation will help to meet agency needs or will hamper the relationship you are expected to establish
   D. Tell her "no" because it is not a good policy to be on such friendly terms with clients

3.____

4. Martha's husband has been arrested in a drug raid and she is extremely anxious. Your supervisor asks that you visit her to determine ways in which the agency may help her. You visit and find her weeping; the house and the children have obviously been neglected.
The BEST thing for you to do is to

    A. tell her to stop crying and help her to clean the apartment and the children
    B. remind her that her husband has been warned and now has to pay for not listening
    C. listen to her, allowing her to express her feelings of fear, loss and grief, and reassure her of your concern
    D. listen to her but caution her that she is neglecting the home and children because of her anxiety and you may have to ask your supervisor to remove the children if she doesn't get any better

4.____

5. Mrs. Dwight's landlord is very slow in making repairs in her apartment. Each time you see her, she complains about this over and over again, calling her landlord names and threatening to report him to the city. She complains to any agency person she meets. Realizing that these complaints are not getting any action, you should

    A. avoid meeting with her because she is annoying
    B. suggest that she see a doctor because she is irrational and should get some help
    C. ask her what she would like to do about the problem and assist her in carrying out her plans
    D. ask the supervisor to see her because you do not have the skills to help her

5.____

6. In the day-to-day operations of the human resources administration, which of the following would you consider to be the PRIMARY function of the agency?

    A. Getting work done to meet city and federal deadlines
    B. Being sure that all of the clients who come to the agency are seen before closing time
    C. Delivering services to those persons who are eligible for assistance
    D. Making sure everyone gets his check on time

6.____

7. During the course of an interview you find it is necessary to arrange a special appointment for the client to return for a further interview. After checking your calendar, you tell the client the date she is to come back. The client, however, says she cannot see you on that date because she is to attend a rally at a community center in her neighborhood.
Of the following, your BEST action should be to

    A. let her know that any other day is an inconvenience to you and remind her that the appointment is for her benefit
    B. forget about the special appointment and try to get along with the information you have
    C. explain to her the need for the appointment and ask when she can meet with you
    D. tell her that since the community center is not city-operated, she must keep her appointment with you

7.____

8. In working with community groups, it is important that you be able to define what a community is.
Of the following definitions, which is the *most appropriate*?
A community

8.____

A. consists of a group of people living fairly close together in a more or less compact territory, who come together in their chief concerns
B. is a particular section of a city designated on a census tract
C. is that portion of a city which constitutes an election district
D. is a section of a city or town in which a particular ethnic group conducts its social, business and religious life

9. The agency has implemented a new policy regarding the intake procedure. You wish to explain and discuss this policy with as many community groups as possible. You make an initial contact by mail.
In order to get your message across well, your letter should be

A. short and as concise as possible explaining why you want to meet with them, and offer several possible times that you will be available
B. short, explaining only that it is important that the groups contact you in order to arrange a meeting
C. drafted by the center's secretary and sent to the usual groups
D. put in the usual announcement form in the center's newsletter

9.____

10. A group of young welfare mothers want to form an organization that will provide baby-sitting services for mothers of children who are too young to enroll in a day care center.
What should be your answer to them?

A. Tell them to try to get the center to change its policy to include young children
B. Arrange the time to meet with them to offer as much advice and support as possible, since most communities do need this service
C. Suggest that it may be better that they spend their time taking care of their own children
D. Ask a social worker to survey the community to determine if such a service is really needed at this time

10.____

11. New regulations have removed the disabled, blind and old age assistance cases from the public assistance caseload. Assistance in these categories is given directly by the federal government. A former client has not received his check. The chairman of the senior citizens committee calls and angrily demands that your agency do something in this man's behalf.
In response you should

A. answer politely, explaining that your agency is not concerned about OAA clients
B. arrange to meet with him in order to discuss the new policy
C. refer him to the Social Security office covering the area where the client lives
D. ask that he call again when he is calmer so that you may discuss this matter with him

11.____

12. A high school student from the community comes to see you about a homework assignment to write a report on your center.
The BEST way to help him is to

A. refer him to a social worker who has daily contact with clients in their homes
B. contact the boy's teacher and find out why you were not warned of his coming
C. explain your center's program and answer as many of his questions as you can
D. give him literature about the welfare system in the city and state

12.____

13. Assume that the women's group of the Community Baptist Church has invited you to a Sunday afternoon service to celebrate the tenth anniversary of the pastor. The agency's relationship with the women is good in that they often offer their homes as emergency homes for adult clients. What should you do about the invitation?

    A. Do not attend but send them a note congratulating the pastor and explaining that agency personnel do not work on Sundays
    B. Ask a social worker who lives close to the church to go
    C. Accept the invitation if at all possible, attend the service and whatever social hour they may have afterwards
    D. Ignore the invitation since this function has little relationship to your job

13.____

14. Suppose that a person you are interviewing becomes angry at some of the questions you have asked, calls you meddlesome and nosy, and states that she will not answer those questions.
Of the following, which is the BEST action for you to take?

    A. Explain the reasons the questions are asked and the importance of the answers
    B. Inform the interviewee that you are only doing your job and advise her that she should answer your questions or leave your office
    C. Report to your supervisor what the interviewee called you and refuse to continue the interview
    D. End the interview and tell the interviewee she will not be serviced by your department

14.____

15. Suppose that during the course of an interview the interviewee demands in a very rude way that she be permitted to talk to your supervisor or someone in charge.
Which of the following is probably the BEST way to handle this situation?

    A. Inform your supervisor of the demand and ask her to speak to the interviewee
    B. Pay no attention to the demands of the interviewee and continue the interview
    C. Report to your supervisor and tell her to get another interviewer for this interviewee
    D. Tell her you are the one "in charge" and that she should talk to you

15.____

16. Suppose that a worker asks a client to answer several required but rather personal questions about the family's health history. The client delays and seems embarrassed about giving the answers.
Of the following, the MOST reasonable response to the client is one which

    A. shows an awareness of the client's efforts to hide something
    B. demonstrates the worker's qualifications for asking such questions
    C. allows this client to be excused from answering the questions
    D. convinces the client that his uneasiness in the situation is understood

16.____

17. A representative from a planned parenthood group comes to see you to get information for a community education program.
You should

    A. check out this group to make sure it is not promoting zero population growth for minority groups
    B. develop a good relationship with him so as to provide better service to clients
    C. make sure they will not encourage unnecessary abortions
    D. refuse to see him

17.____

18. A member of a clerical training program is continually late to classes. He explains to you that he has a hard time getting up and asks that you report him on time because he needs to train for a job.
What should your response be?

    A. Tell him that you get there on time and so should he
    B. Tell him that you do not lie for anyone
    C. Explain that it is your duty to keep accurate records and refer him to a counselor
    D. Tell him that you will cooperate with him but he has to try to do better

18.____

19. In a community meeting to explain a new agency policy, you find that the audience has no questions about the policy or your explanations.
What would be the *most appropriate* response to the silence?

    A. Leave right away before they think of questions
    B. Thank the audience for their attention and assure them that you will be available if there are any questions later
    C. Ask several members in the audience if they understand the new policy
    D. Explain that the audience could not possibly understand all of the policy and they must have questions

19.____

20. Assume that you are confronted by an angry member of the public who has not been able to obtain the information he needs from your office. You do not know the answer to his question.
The BEST thing for you to do would be to

    A. tell him to come back another time, after you have looked up the information
    B. check with your supervisor to find the correct answer
    C. tell him to ask in another office, so that you will not lose time looking for the information
    D. make up an answer to keep the man satisfied until the right answer is found

20.____

KEY (CORRECT ANSWERS)

1. C		11. C
2. D		12. C
3. C		13. C
4. C		14. A
5. C		15. A
6. C		16. D
7. C		17. B
8. A		18. C
9. A		19. B
10. B		20. B

READING COMPREHENSION
UNDERSTANDING AND INTERPRETING WRITTEN MATERIAL

EXAMINATION SECTION
TEST 1

DIRECTIONS: Each question or incomplete statement is followed by several suggested answers or completions. Select the one that BEST answers the question or completes the statement. *PRINT THE LETTER OF THE CORRECT ANSWER IN THE SPACE AT THE RIGHT.*

Questions 1-4.

DIRECTIONS: Questions 1 through 4 are to be answered SOLELY on the basis of the information in the following paragraphs.

Some authorities have questioned whether the term *culture of poverty* should be used since *culture* means a design for living which is passed down from generation to generation. The culture of poverty is, however, a very useful concept if it is used with care, with recognition that poverty is a subculture, and with avoidance of the *cookie-cutter* approach. With regard to the individual, the cookie-cutter view assumes that all individuals in a culture turn out exactly alike, as if they were so many cookies. It overlooks the fact that, at least in our urban society, every individual is a member of more than one subculture; and which subculture most strongly influences his response in a given situation depends on the interaction of a great many factors, including his individual make-up and history, the specifics of the various subcultures to which he belongs, and the specifics of the given situation. It is always important to avoid the cookie-cutter view of culture, with regard to the individual and to the culture or subculture involved.

With regard to the culture as a whole, the cookie-cutter concept again assumes homogeneity and consistency. It forgets that within any one culture or subculture there are conflicts and contradictions, and that at any given moment an individual may have to choose, consciously, between conflicting values or patterns. Also, most individuals, in varying degrees, have a dual set of values—those by which they live and those they cherish as best. This point has been made and documented repeatedly about the culture of poverty.

1. The *cookie-cutter* approach assumes that   1.____

    A. members of the same *culture* are all alike
    B. *culture* stays the same from generation to generation
    C. the term *culture* should not be applied to groups who are poor
    D. there are value conflicts within most *cultures*

2. According to the above passage, every person in our cities   2.____

    A. is involved in the conflicts of urban culture
    B. recognizes that poverty is a subculture
    C. lives by those values to which he is exposed
    D. belongs to more than one subculture

3. The above passage emphasizes that a culture is likely to contain within it   3.____

    A. one dominant set of values
    B. a number of contradictions
    C. one subculture to which everyone belongs
    D. members who are exactly alike

4. According to the above passage, individuals are sometimes forced to choose BETWEEN   4.____

    A. cultures
    B. subcultures
    C. different sets of values
    D. a new culture and an old culture

Questions 5-8.

DIRECTIONS: Questions 5 through 8 are to be answered SOLELY on the basis of the following passage.

There are approximately 33 million poor people in the United States; 14.3 million of them are children, 5.3 million are old people, and the remainder are in other categories. Altogether, 6.5 million families live in poverty because the heads of the households cannot work; they are either too old or too sick or too severely handicapped, or they are widowed or deserted mothers of young children. There are the working poor: the low-paid workers, the workers in seasonal industries, and soldiers with no additional income who are heads of families. There are the underemployed: those who would like full-time jobs but cannot find them, those employees who would like year-round work but lack the opportunity, and those who are employed below their level of training. There are the non-working poor: the older men and women with small retirement incomes and those with no income, the disabled, the physically and mentally handicapped, and the chronically sick.

5. According to the above passage, approximately what percent of the poor people in the United States are children?   5.____

    A. 33   B. 16   C. 20   D. 44

6. According to the above passage, people who work in seasonal industries are LIKELY to be classified as   6.____

    A. working poor   B. underemployed
    C. non-working poor   D. low-paid workers

7. According to the above passage, the category of non-working poor includes people who   7.____

    A. receive unemployment insurance
    B. cannot find full-time work
    C. are disabled or mentally handicapped
    D. are soldiers with wives and children

8. According to the above passage, among the underemployed are those who   8.____

    A. can find only part-time work
    B. are looking for their first jobs
    C. are inadequately trained
    D. depend on insufficient retirement incomes

Questions 9-13.

DIRECTIONS: Read the Inter-office Memo below. Then answer Questions 9 through 13 SOLELY on the basis of the memo.

INTER-OFFICE MEMORANDUM

To: Alma Robinson, Human Resources Aide

From: Frank Shields, Social Worker

I would like to have you help Mr. Edward Tunney who is trying to raise his two children by himself. He needs to learn to improve the physical care of his children and especially of his daughter Helen, age 9. She is avoided and ridiculed at school because her hair is uncombed, her teeth not properly cleaned, her clothing torn, wrinkled and dirty, as well as shabby and poorly fitted. The teachers and school officials have contacted the Department and the social worker for two years about Helen. She is not able to make friends because of these problems. I have talked to Mr. Tunney about improvements for the child's clothing, hair, and hygiene. He tends to deny these things are problems, but is cooperative, and a second person showing him the importance of better physical care for Helen would be helpful.

Perhaps you could teach Helen how to fix her own hair. She has all the materials. I would also like you to form your own opinion of the sanitary conditions in the home and how they could be improved.

Mr. Tunney is expecting your visit and is willing to talk with you about ways he can help with these problems.

9.   In the above memorandum, the Human Resources Aide is being asked to help Mr. Tunney to   9._____

   A.   improve the learning habits of his children
   B.   enable his children to make friends at school
   C.   take responsibility for the upbringing of his children
   D.   give attention to the grooming and cleanliness of his children

10.   This case was brought to the attention of the social worker by   10._____

   A.   government officials
   B.   teachers and school officials
   C.   the Department
   D.   Mr. Tunney

11.   In general, Mr. Tunney's attitude with regard to his children could BEST be described as   11._____

   A.   interested in correcting the obvious problems, but unable to do so alone
   B.   unwilling to follow the advice of those who are trying to help
   C.   concerned but unaware of the seriousness of these problems
   D.   interested in helping them, but afraid of taking the advice of the social worker

12. Which of the following actions has NOT been suggested as a possible step for the   12._____
Human Resources Aide to take?

    A. Help Helen to learn to care for herself by teaching her grooming skills
    B. Determine ways of improvement through information gathered on a home visit
    C. Discuss her own views on Helen's problems with school officials
    D. Ask Mr. Tunney in what ways he believes the physical care may be improved

13. According to the above memo, the Human Resources Aide is ESPECIALLY being asked   13._____
to observe and form her own opinions about

    A. the relationship between Mr. Tunney and the school officials
    B. Helen's attitude toward her classmates and teacher
    C. the sanitary conditions in the home
    D. the reasons Mr. Tunney is not cooperative with the agency

Questions 14-16.

DIRECTIONS: Questions 14 through 16 are to be answered SOLELY on the basis of the following paragraph.

    In social work, professional responsibility and accountability extend to a larger segment
of the general community than is true of the older professions which have more limited and
more specialized areas of community responsibility and public trust. Advances in knowledge
about both the nature of human institutions and the nature of the individual have placed social
work in the center of a vast complex of interrelationships. The situations that come to the
attention of the social worker, whatever his functions, may be the circumstances of an individual client or of a group or of a community which may or may not be socially sanctioned, and
the proposed remedy may be considered desirable or questionable. When there is agreement between the client group and the community on the nature of the problem and on the
validity of the proposed remedy, such agreement may lead to the establishment of social institutions. Complications arise when the client or client group, or the community, does not
accept the need for change or is not in agreement with the social worker about the direction it
should take. The social worker has the obligation to pursue his objective regardless of the difficulties. Even if social work, as it is practiced today, were to achieve the degree of acceptance afforded the older professions, it would still find itself, with every new development,
holding unorthodox and not very respectable views on many aspects of personal and social
relationships.

14. The MOST accurate of the following statements about the relationship between social   14._____
work and the other professions is:

    A. Advances in knowledge have placed social work in a central position among the
professions
    B. Although younger, social work has become basic to the older professions in their
responsibility and accountability in the community
    C. It is the responsibility of social workers to hold unorthodox views on social relation-
ships
    D. The areas of responsibility of social work within the community are more extensive
than those of the older professions

15. When, because of an existing problem, a social worker has advocated a change in a   15.____
    social institution which has been opposed by the community, the social worker should

    A. attempt to surmount the opposition, continuing to seek to reach his objective
    B. change his position to gain the support of the community
    C. review the position that he has taken to see whether he cannot revise his objective
       to the point where it may gain community support
    D. work to achieve for his profession the degree of acceptance which is afforded the
       older professions

16. Of the following, the BEST title for the above paragraph is   16.____

    A. DANGERS OF SOCIAL RESPONSIBILITY
    B. SOCIAL WORK AND THE OLDER PROFESSIONS COMPARED
    C. SOCIAL WORKERS' RESPONSIBILITY IN SOCIAL CHANGE
    D. UNORTHODOX SOCIAL WORK

Questions 17-19.

DIRECTIONS: Questions 17 through 19 are to be answered SOLELY on the basis of the fol-
               lowing paragraph.

Toward the end of the 19th century, as social work principles and theories took form,
areas of conflict between the responsibility of the social worker to the client group and to the
status quo of social and economic institutions became highlighted. The lay public's attitude
toward the individual poor was one of emphasis on betterment through the development of
the individual's capacity for self-maintenance. They hoped to maintain this end both by helping the client to rely on his unused capacities for self-help and by facilitating his access to
what were assumed to be the natural sources of help family, relatives, churches, and other
charitable associations. Professional social workers were fast becoming aware of the need for
social reform. They perceived that traditional methods of help were largely inadequate to
cope with the factors that were creating poverty and maladjustment for a large number of the
population faster than the charity societies could relieve such problems through individual
effort. The critical view, held by social workers, of the character of many social institutions
was not shared by other groups in the community who had not reached the same point of
awareness about the deficiencies in the functioning of these institutions. Thus, the views of
the social worker were beginning to differ, sometimes radically, from the basic views of large
sections of the population.

17. The social workers of the late 19th century found themselves in conflict with the status   17.____
    quo CHIEFLY because they

    A. had become professionalized through the development of a body of theory and
       principles
    B. became aware that many social ills could not be cured through existing institutions
    C. felt that traditional methods of helping the poor must be expanded regardless of the
       cost to the public
    D. believed that the right of the individual to be self-determining should be empha-
       sized

18. It was becoming apparent, by the end of the 19th century, that in relation to the needs of   18.____
    the poor, existing social institutions

A. did not sufficiently emphasize the ability of the poor to utilize their natural sources of help
B. were using the proper methods of helping the poor, but were hindered by the work of social workers who had broken with tradition
C. were no longer capable of meeting the needs of the poor because the causes of poverty had changed
D. were capable of meeting the needs of the poor, but needed more financial aid from the general public since the number of people in need had increased

19. Social workers at the end of the 19th century may be PROPERLY classified as   19._____

A. growing in awareness that many social ills could be alleviated through social reform
B. very perceptive individuals who realized that traditional methods of help were humiliating to the poor
C. strong advocates of expanding the existing traditional sources of relief
D. too radical because they favored easing life for the poor at the expense of increased taxation to the public at large

Questions 20-24.

DIRECTIONS: Questions 20 through 24 are to be answered SOLELY on the basis of the following paragraphs.

With the generation gap yawning before us, it is well to remember that 20 years ago teenagers produced a larger proportion of unwedlock births than today, and that the illegitimacy rate among teenagers is lower than among women in their twenties and thirties. In addition, the illegitimacy rate has risen less among teenagers than among older women.

It is helpful to note the difference between illegitimacy rate and illegitimacy ratio. The ratio is the number of illegitimate babies per 1,000 live births. The rate is the number of illegitimate births per 1,000 unmarried women of childbearing age. The ratio talks about babies; the rate talks about mothers. The ratio is useful for planning services, but worse than useless for considering trends since it depends on the age and marital <u>composition</u> of the population, illegitimacy rate, and the fertility of married women. For example, the ratio among girls under 18 is bound to be high in comparison with older women since few are married mothers. However, the illegitimacy rate is relatively low.

20. Of the following, the MOST suitable title for the above passage would be   20._____

A. THE GENERATION GAP
B. MORAL STANDARDS AND TEENAGE ILLEGITIMACY RATIO
C. A COMPARISON OF ILLEGITIMACY RATE AND ILLEGITIMACY RATIO
D. CAUSES OF HIGH ILLEGITIMACY RATES

21. According to the above passage, which of the following statements is CORRECT?   21._____
The illegitimacy

A. rate has fallen among women in their thirties
B. ratio is the number of illegitimate births per 1,000 unmarried women of childbearing age

C. ratio is partially dependent on the illegitimacy rate
D. rate is more useful than the ratio for planning services

22. According to the above passage, of the following age groups, the illegitimacy ratio would be expected to be HIGHEST in comparison with the other groups for the group aged   22.____

    A. 17   B. 21   C. 25   D. 29

23. According to the above passage, of the following age groups, the illegitimacy rate would be expected to be LOWEST in comparison with the other groups for the group aged   23.____

    A. 17   B. 21   C. 25   D. 29

24. As used in the above passage, the underlined word composition means MOST NEARLY   24.____

    A. essay   B. makeup
    C. security   D. happiness

25. A document was published by a public agency and distributed for discussion. The document contained data showing trends in the level of reading among freshmen college students and suggested that the high schools were not investing enough effort in overcoming retardation. It compared the costs of intensifying reading instruction in the secondary schools as compared to costs in colleges for such instruction.   25.____
    According to the above statement, it is REASONABLE to conclude that

    A. the document proposed new programs
    B. the college students read better than high school students
    C. some college students need remedial reading
    D. the study was done by a consultant

KEY (CORRECT ANSWERS)

1.	A	11.	C
2.	D	12.	C
3.	B	13.	C
4.	C	14.	D
5.	D	15.	A
6.	A	16.	C
7.	C	17.	B
8.	A	18.	C
9.	D	19.	A
10.	B	20.	C

21.	C
22.	A
23.	A
24.	B
25.	C

TEST 2

DIRECTIONS: Each question or incomplete statement is followed by several suggested answers or completions. Select the one that BEST answers the question or completes the statement. *PRINT THE LETTER OF THE CORRECT ANSWER IN THE SPACE AT THE RIGHT.*

Questions 1-4.

DIRECTIONS: Questions 1 through 4 are to be answered SOLELY on the basis of the following paragraph.

Form W-280 provides a uniform standard for estimating family expenses and is used as a basis for determining eligibility for the care of children at public expense. The extent to which legally responsible relatives can pay for the care of a child must be computed. The minimum amount of the payment required from legally responsible relatives shall be 50% of the budget surplus as computed on Form W-281, plus any governmental benefits, such as OASDI benefits, or Railroad Retirement benefits being paid to a family member for the child receiving care or services. Because of the kinds and quantities of services included in the budget schedule (W-280) and because only 50% of the budget surplus is required as payment, no allowances for special needs are made, except for verified payments into civil service pension funds, amounts paid to a garnishee, or amounts paid to another agency for the care of other relatives for whom the relative is legally responsible, or for other such expenses if approval has been granted after Form W-278 has been submitted. In determining the income of the legally responsible relative, income from wages, self-employment, unemployment insurance benefits, and any such portion of governmental benefits as is not specifically designated for children already receiving care is to be included. Should 50% of the family's surplus meet the child care expenses, the case shall not be processed. Form W-279, an agreement to support, shall be signed by the legally responsible relative when 50% of the surplus is $1.00 or more a week.

1. A family is required to sign an agreement to support   1.____

    A. whenever they are legally responsible for the support of the child under care
    B. before any care at public expense is given to the child
    C. when their income surplus is at least $2.00/week
    D. when 50% of their income surplus meets the full needs of the child

2. The reason for allowing a family to deduct only certain specified expenses when computing the amount they are able to contribute to the support of a child being cared for at public expense is that the family   2.____

    A. should not be permitted to have a higher standard of living than the child being cared for
    B. the budget schedule is sufficiently generous and includes an allowance for other unusual expenses
    C. may not be able to verify their extraordinary expenses
    D. may meet other unusual expenses from the remainder of their surplus

3. Mrs. B wishes to have her daughter Mary cared for at public expense. Her income includes her wages and OASDI benefits of $250 a month, of which $50 a month is paid for Mary and $50 a month for another minor member of the family who is already being cared for at public expense. In order to determine the amount of Mrs. B's budget surplus, it is necessary to consider as income her wages and   3.____

    A. $ 50 of OASDI received for Mary
    B. $150 of the OASDI benefits
    C. $200 of the OASDI benefits
    D. $200 of the OASDI benefits if she is legally responsible for the care of the other child in placement

4. In order to determine a family's ability to contribute to the support of a child, the worker should   4.____

    A. have the legally responsible member sign Form W-279 agreeing to support the child, and then compute the family surplus on W-281 in accordance with public assistance standards
    B. compute the family's income in accordance with the allowance included on Form W-280 and the expenses included on Form W-278 and have Form W-279 signed if necessary
    C. use Form W-278 to work out a budget schedule for the family and compute their surplus on W-281 and then have them sign W-279 if necessary
    D. compute income and expenses on Form W-281, based on Form W-280, and have Form W-279 signed if necessary

Questions 5-10.

DIRECTIONS: Questions 5 through 10 are to be answered SOLELY on the basis of the following passage.

Too often in the past, society has accepted the existing social welfare programs, preferring to tinker with refinements when fundamental reform was in order. It has been a demeaning, degrading welfare system in which the instrument of government was wrongfully and ineptly used. It has been a system which has only alienated those forced to benefit from it and demoralized those who had to administer it at the level where the pain was clearly visible.

There is a need to put this nation on a course in which cash benefits, providing a basic level of support, are conferred in such a way as to intrude as little as possible into privacy and self-respect. It is difficult to define a basic level of support, no matter how high or low it might be set. In the end, however, the decision is not determined so much by how much is truly adequate for a family to meet all of its needs, but by the resources available to carry out the promise. That may be a harsh fact of life but it is also just that – a fact of life.

5. Of the following, the MOST suitable title for the above passage would be   5.____

    A. THE NEED FOR GOVERNMENT CONTROL OF WELFARE
    B. DETERMINING THE BASIC LEVEL OF SUPPORT
    C. THE NEED FOR WELFARE REFORM
    D. THE ELIMINATION OF WELFARE PROGRAMS

6. In the above passage, the author's GREATEST criticism of the welfare system is that it is too   6.____

    A. disrespectful of recipients
    B. expensive to administer
    C. limited by regulations
    D. widespread in application

7. According to the above passage, the BASIC level of support is actually determined by   7.____

    A. how much is required for a family to meet all of its needs
    B. the age of the recipients
    C. how difficult it is to administer the program
    D. the economic resources of the nation

8. In the above passage, the author does NOT argue for   8.____

    A. a work incentive system   B. a basic level of support
    C. cash benefits   D. the privacy of recipients

9. As used in the above passage, the underlined word demeaning means MOST NEARLY   9.____

    A. ineffective   B. expensive
    C. overburdened   D. humiliating

10. As used in the above passage, the underlined word ineptly means MOST NEARLY   10.____

    A. foolishly   B. unsuccessfully
    C. unskillfully   D. unhappily

Questions 11-14.

DIRECTIONS: Questions 11 through 14 are to be answered SOLELY on the basis of the following paragraph.

    The unemployment rate, which counts those unemployed in the sense that they are actively looking for work and unable to find it, gives a relatively superficial index of economic conditions in a community. A better index is the subemployment rate which includes the unemployment rate and also includes those working part-time while they are trying to get full-time work; those heads of households under 65 years of age who earn less than $240 per week working full-time, and those individuals under 65 who are not heads of households and earn less than $224 per week in a full-time job; and an estimate of the males *not counted,* which is a very real concern in ghetto areas.

11. Of the following, the MOST suitable title for the above paragraph would be   11.____

    A. EMPLOYMENT IN THE UNITED STATES
    B. PART-TIME WORKERS AND THE ECONOMY
    C. THE LABOR MARKET AND THE COMMUNITY
    D. TWO INDICATORS OF ECONOMIC CONDITIONS

12. On the basis of the above paragraph, which of the following statements is CORRECT?   12.____

    A. The unemployment rate includes everyone who is not fully employed.
    B. The subemployment rate is higher than the unemployment rate.

C. The unemployment rate gives a more complete picture of the economic situation than the subemployment rate.
D. The subemployment rate indicates how many part-time workers are dissatisfied with the number of hours they work per week.

13. As used in the above paragraph, the underlined word <u>superficial</u> means MOST NEARLY   13.____

    A. exaggerated   B. official
    C. surface   D. current

14. According to the above paragraph, which of the following is included in the subemployment rate?   14.____

    A. Everyone who is unemployed
    B. All part-time workers
    C. Everyone under 65 who earns less than $220 per week in a full-time job
    D. All heads of households who earn less than $240 per week in a full-time job

Questions 15-16.

DIRECTIONS: Questions 15 and 16 are to be answered SOLELY on the basis of the following paragraphs.

The city's economy has its own dynamics, and there is only so much the government can do to shape it. But that margin is critically important. If the city uses its points of leverage, it can generate a large number of jobs – and good jobs, jobs that lead to advancement.

As a major employer itself, the city can upgrade the jobs it offers and greatly improve its services to the public if it does so. Since highly skilled professionals will always be in short supply, the city must train more paraprofessionals to take over routine tasks. Equally important, it must provide them with a realistic job ladder so they can move on up – nurse's aide to certified nurse, for example, teacher's aide to teacher. The training programs for such upgrading will require a substantial public investment but the cost-benefit return should be excellent.

As a major purchaser of goods and services, the city can stimulate business enterprise in the ghetto. The growth of Black and Puerto Rican firms will produce more local jobs; it will also create the kind of managerial talent the ghetto needs.

New kinds of enterprise can be set up. In housing, for example, there is a huge backlog of rehabilitation work to be done and a large pool of unskilled manpower to be trained for it. Corporations can be formed to take over tenements, remodel, maintain, and operate them, as in the Brownsville Home Maintenance Program. Grocery cooperatives to bring food prices down are another possibility.

15. According to the above paragraphs, the city is the major employer and by using its capacity it can   15.____

    A. assist unskilled people with talent to move up on the job ladder
    B. create private enterprises that will renew all areas of the city in need of renewal
    C. eliminate poverty in the ghetto areas by selective purchase of goods and services
    D. have no influence on the economy of the city

16. According to the above paragraph, one may REASONABLY conclude that   16.____

    A. the city has no power to influence the job market
    B. a byproduct of strategic purchasing and employment and training practices can be the rehabilitation of housing and the lowering of food prices
    C. highly skilled professions, which are now in short supply, will no longer be needed after paraprofes-sionals are trained to take over routine jobs
    D. the city's major objective is to bring down food prices

Questions 17-21.

DIRECTIONS: Questions 17 through 21 are statements based on the following paragraphs. For each question, there are two statements.

    Based on the information in the paragraphs, mark your answer A, B, or C, as follows.
        A. If only statement 1 is correct;
        B. If only statement 2 is correct;
        C. If both statements are correct.
    Mark your answer D if the excerpts do not contain sufficient evidence for concluding whether either or both statements are correct.

Upstate, 35% of the AFDC families lived in districts suburban to New York City, 43% in upstate urban districts, and 22% in the rest of upstate. Among white families, 28% resided in suburban districts, 40% in upstate urban districts, and 32% in the rest of upstate. Among non-white families, 43% lived in suburban districts, 47% in upstate urban districts, and 10% in the rest of upstate.

Upstate, 78.7% of the AFDC families resided in SMSA (Standard Metropolitan Statistical Area) counties, including 68.7% of the whites and 90.4% of the non-whites. In Buffalo, 83.3% of the families were non-white; in Rochester, 57.9% were non-whites; in cities of 100,000 to 250,000 (Albany, Syracuse, and Utica), 55.2% were white; and in the rest of the upstate urban counties, 86.5% were white.

The two most frequent underlying reasons for a family requiring AFDC were desertion of the father (31.3% of the cases) and *father not married to mother* (30.3%). Desertions were proportionately highest among Puerto Rican families (38.6%), compared with 29.4% for Blacks and 23.6% for white families. Unmarried mothers comprised 39.4% of the Black cases, compared with 26.6% for Puerto Ricans and 14.8% for white cases.

White families had substantially higher proportions in the separated and divorced categories than non-whites. When the deserted, separated, and divorced categories are combined, marital breakdown occurred in 59% of the white AFDC families, compared with 52.3% for Puerto Ricans and 44.4% for Blacks.

Substantial ethnic differences existed in the proportions of incapacitated fathers; overall, the rate was 7.5%, but among white families the rate was 14.8%, compared with 9.4% for Puerto Ricans and only 3.0% for Blacks. Families where the father was deceased comprised 5.9% of the AFDC cases.

In New York City, desertion rates (35.3% of all cases) were substantially higher than upstate (18.9%), particularly among white families, as ethnic differences in New York City diminished considerably. Unmarried mother rates closely paralleled the statewide figures.

Incapacity of the father occurred more frequently among white families upstate (17.5%) than among white families in New York City (10.4%). Deceased fathers were proportionately highest among the New York City Black and Puerto Rican caseload, possibly reflecting fewer remarriage and employment opportunities among these groups in the event of the death of the father.

17.
1. The most frequent underlying reason for a family requiring AFDC was *father not married to mother*.
2. Three-fourths of New York State's AFDC families lived in New York City.

17._____

18.
1. There were more cases of desertion among AFDC cases upstate than there were of incapacity of the father among white AFDC families upstate.
2. There was a higher percentage of marital breakdowns among white AFDC families compared to Puerto Rican or Black families.

18._____

19.
1. Desertion of the father accounted for more AFDC cases than all other reasons combined.
2. The proportion of incapacitated fathers in Puerto Rican families was higher than the overall rate of incapacitated fathers.

19._____

20.
1. Non-white families had substantially higher proportions in the divorced and separated categories than white families.
2. Among AFDC families in New York State, there were more Puerto Ricans than Blacks in the combined deserted, separated, and divorced categories.

20._____

21.
1. In New York City, there was a higher percentage of unmarried mothers among Puerto Rican AFDC families than among white cases.
2. Among white families, desertion rates were considerably higher upstate than in New York City.

21._____

Questions 22-25.

DIRECTIONS: Questions 22 through 25 are to be answered SOLELY on the basis of information given in the following paragraph.

The question of what material is relevant is not as simple as it might seem. Frequently, material which seems irrelevant to the inexperienced has, because of the common tendency to disguise and distort and misplace one's feelings, considerable significance. It may be necessary to let the client *ramble on* for a while in order to clear the decks, as it were, so that he may get down to things that really are on his mind. On the other hand, with an already disturbed person, it may be important for the interviewer to know when to discourage further elaboration of upsetting material. This is especially the case where the worker would be unable to do anything about it. An inexperienced interviewer might, for instance, be intrigued with the bizarre elaboration of material that the psychotic produces, but further elaboration of this might encourage the client in his instability. A too random discussion may indicate that the interviewee is not certain in what areas the interviewer is prepared to help him, and he may be seeking some direction. Or again, satisfying though it may be for the interviewer to have the interviewee tell him intimate details, such revelations sometimes need to be checked or encouraged only in small doses. An interviewee who has *talked too much* often reveals subsequent anxiety. This is illustrated by the fact that frequently after a *confessional* interview, the interviewee surprises the interviewer by being withdrawn, inarticulate, or hostile, or by breaking the next appointment.

22. Sometimes a client may reveal certain personal information to an interviewer and subsequently may feel anxious about this revelation.
    If, during an interview, a client begins to discuss very personal matters, it would be BEST to

    A. tell the client, in no uncertain terms, that you're not interested in personal details
    B. ignore the client at this point
    C. encourage the client to elaborate further on the details
    D. inform the client that the information seems to be very personal

22.____

23. The author indicates that clients with severe psychological disturbances pose an especially difficult problem for the inexperienced interviewer.
    The DIFFICULTY lies in the possibility of the client

    A. becoming physically violent and harming the interviewer
    B. *rambling on* for a while
    C. revealing irrelevant details which may be followed by cancelled appointments
    D. reverting to an unstable state as a result of interview material

23.____

24. An interviewer should be constantly alert to the possibility of obtaining clues from the client as to the problem areas.
    According to the above passage, a client who discusses topics at random may be

    A. unsure of what problems the interviewer can provide help
    B. reluctant to discuss intimate details
    C. trying to impress the interviewer with his knowledge
    D. deciding what relevant material to elaborate on

24.____

25. The evaluation of a client's responses may reveal substantial information that may aid the interviewer in assessing the problem areas that are of concern to the client. Responses that seemed irrelevant at the time of the interview may be of significance because

    A. considerable significance is attached to all irrelevant material
    B. emotional feelings are frequently masked
    C. an initial *rambling on* is often a prelude to what is actually bothering the client
    D. disturbed clients often reveal subsequent anxiety

25.____

KEY (CORRECT ANSWERS)

1.	C	11.	D
2.	D	12.	B
3.	B	13.	C
4.	D	14.	C
5.	C	15.	A
6.	A	16.	B
7.	D	17.	D
8.	A	18.	C
9.	D	19.	B
10.	C	20.	D

21.	A
22.	D
23.	D
24.	A
25.	B

———

INTERVIEWING
EXAMINATION SECTION
TEST 1

DIRECTIONS: Each question or incomplete statement is followed by several suggested answers or completions. Select the one that BEST answers the question or completes the statement. *PRINT THE LETTER OF THE CORRECT ANSWER IN THE SPACE AT THE RIGHT.*

1. An interview is BEST conducted in private primarily because   1._____

    A. the person interviewed will tend to be less self-conscious
    B. the interviewer will be able to maintain his continuity of thought better
    C. it will insure that the interview is "off the record"
    D. people tend to "show off" before an audience

2. An interviewer can BEST establish a good relationship with the person being interviewed by   2._____

    A. assuming casual interest in the statements made by the person being interviewed
    B. taking the point of view of the person interviewed
    C. controlling the interview to a major extent
    D. showing a genuine interest in the person

3. An interviewer will be better able to understand the person interviewed and his problems if he recognizes that much of the person's behavior is due to motives   3._____

    A. which are deliberate
    B. of which he is unaware
    C. which are inexplicable
    D. which are kept under control

4. An interviewer's attention must be directed toward himself as well as toward the person interviewed. This statement means that the interviewer should   4._____

    A. keep in mind the extent to which his own prejudices may influence his judgment
    B. rationalize the statements made by the person interviewed
    C. gain the respect and confidence of the person interviewed
    D. avoid being too impersonal

5. More complete expression will be obtained from a person being interviewed if the interviewer can create the impression that   5._____

    A. the data secured will become part of a permanent record
    B. official information must be accurate in every detail
    C. it is the duty of the person interviewed to give accurate data
    D. the person interviewed is participating in a discussion of his own problems

6. The practice of asking leading questions should be avoided in an interview because the   6._____

    A. interviewer risks revealing his attitudes to the person being interviewed
    B. interviewer may be led to ignore the objective attitudes of the person interviewed
    C. answers may be unwarrantedly influenced
    D. person interviewed will resent the attempt to lead him and will be less cooperative

7. A good technique for the interviewer to use in an effort to secure reliable data and to reduce the possibility of misunderstanding is to

    7.____

    A. use casual undirected conversation, enabling the person being interviewed to talk about himself, and thus secure the desired information
    B. adopt the procedure of using direct questions regularly
    C. extract the desired information from the person being interviewed by putting him on the defensive
    D. explain to the person being interviewed the information desired and the reason for needing it

8. You are interviewing a patient to determine whether she is eligible for medical assistance. Of the many questions that you have to ask her, some are routine questions that patients tend to answer willingly and easily. Other questions are more personal and some patients tend to resent being asked them and avoid answering them directly. For you to begin the interview with the more personal questions would be

    8.____

    A. *desirable,* because the end of the interview will go smoothly and the patient will be left with a warm feeling
    B. *undesirable,* because the patient might not know the answers to the questions
    C. *desirable,* because you will be able to return to these questions later to verify the accuracy of the responses
    D. *undesirable,* because you might antagonize the patient before you have had a chance to establish rapport

9. While interviewing a patient about her family composition, the patient asks you whether you are married.
Of the following, the MOST appropriate way for you to handle this situation is to

    9.____

    A. answer the question briefly and redirect her back to the topic under discussion
    B. refrain from answering the question and proceed with the interview
    C. advise the patient that it is more important that she answer your questions than that you answer hers, and proceed with the interview
    D. promise the patient that you will answer her question later, in the hope that she will forget, and redirect her back to the topic under discussion

10. In response to a question about his employment history, a patient you are interviewing rambles and talks about unrelated matters.
Of the following, the MOST appropriate course of action for you to take FIRST is to

    10.____

    A. ask questions to direct the patient back to his employment history
    B. advise him to concentrate on your questions and not to discuss irrelevant information
    C. ask him why he is resisting a discussion of his employment history
    D. advise him that if you cannot get the information you need, he will not be eligible for medical assistance

11. Suppose that a person you are interviewing becomes angry at some of the questions   11.____
    you have asked, calls you meddlesome and nosy, and states that she will not answer
    those questions.
    Of the following, which is the BEST action for you to take?

    A. Explain the reasons the questions are asked and the importance of the answers.
    B. Inform the interviewee that you are only doing your job and advise her that she
       should answer your questions or leave the office.
    C. Report to your supervisor what the interviewee called you and refuse to continue
       the interview.
    D. End the interview and tell the interviewee she will not be serviced by your depart-
       ment.

12. Suppose that during the course of an interview the interviewee demands in a very rude   12.____
    way that she be permitted to talk to your supervisor or someone in charge.
    Which of the following is probably the BEST way to handle this situation?

    A. Inform your supervisor of the demand and ask her to speak to the interviewee.
    B. Pay no attention to the demands of the interviewee and continue the interview.
    C. Report to your supervisor and tell her to get another interviewer for this inter-
       viewee.
    D. Tell her you are the one "in charge" and that she should talk to you.

13. Of the following, the outcome of an interview by an aide depends MOST heavily on the   13.____

    A. personality of the interviewee
    B. personality of the aide
    C. subject matter of the questions asked
    D. interaction between aide and interviewee

14. Some patients being interviewed are primarily interested in making a favorable impres-   14.____
    sion. The aide should be aware of the fact that such patients are more likely than other
    patients to

    A. try to anticipate the answers the interviewer is looking for
    B. answer all questions openly and frankly
    C. try to assume the role of interviewer
    D. be anxious to get the interview over as quickly as possible

15. The type of interview which an aide usually conducts is substantially different from most   15.____
    interviewing situations in all of the following aspects EXCEPT the

    A. setting   B. kinds of clients
    C. techniques employed   D. kinds of problems

16. During an interview, an aide uses a "leading question." This type of question is so-called   16.____
    because it generally

    A. starts a series of questions about one topic
    B. suggests the answer which the aide wants
    C. forms the basis for a following "trick" question
    D. sets, at the beginning, the tone of the interview

17. Casework interviewing is always directed to the client and his situation. The one of the following which is the MOST accurate statement with respect to the proper focus of an interview is that the

    A. caseworker limits the client to concentration on objective data
    B. client is generally permitted to talk about facts and feelings with no direction from the caseworker
    C. main focus in casework interviews is on feelings rather than facts
    D. caseworker is responsible for helping the client focus on any material which seems to be related to his problems or difficulties

17.____

18. Assume that you are conducting a training program for the caseworkers under your supervision. At one of the sessions, you discuss the problem of interviewing a dull and stupid client who gives a slow and disconnected case history. The BEST of the following interviewing methods for you to recommend in such a case in order to ascertain the facts is for the caseworker to

    A. ask the client leading questions requiring "yes" or "no" answers
    B. request the client to limit his narration to the essential facts so that the interview can be kept as brief as possible
    C. review the story with the client, patiently asking simple questions
    D. tell the client that unless he is more cooperative he cannot be helped to solve his problem

18.____

19. A recent development in casework interviewing procedure, known as multiple-client interviewing, consists of interviews of the entire family at the same time. However, this may not be an effective casework method in certain situations. Of the following, the situation in which the standard individual interview would be preferable is when

    A. family members derive consistent and major gratification from assisting each other in their destructive responses
    B. there is a crucial family conflict to which the members are reacting
    C. the family is overwhelmed by interpersonal anxieties which have not been explored
    D. the worker wants to determine the pattern of family interaction to further his diagnostic understanding

19.____

20. A follow-up interview was arranged for an applicant in order that he could furnish certain requested evidence. At this follow-up interview, the applicant still fails to furnish the necessary evidence. It would be MOST advisable for you to

    A. advise the applicant that he is now considered ineligible
    B. ask the applicant how soon he can get the necessary evidence and set a date for another interview
    C. question the applicant carefully and thoroughly to determine if he has misrepresented or falsified any information
    D. set a date for another interview and tell the applicant to get the necessary evidence by that time.

20.____

KEY (CORRECT ANSWERS)

1.	A	11.	A
2.	D	12.	A
3.	B	13.	D
4.	A	14.	A
5.	D	15.	C
6.	C	16.	B
7.	D	17.	D
8.	D	18.	C
9.	A	19.	A
10.	A	20.	B

———

TEST 2

DIRECTIONS: Each question or incomplete statement is followed by several suggested answers or completions. Select the one that BEST answers the question or completes the statement. *PRINT THE LETTER OF THE CORRECT ANSWER IN THE SPACE AT THE RIGHT.*

1. In interviewing, the practice of anticipating an applicant's answers to questions is generally

    A. *desirable,* because it is effective and economical when it is necessary to interview large numbers of applicants
    B. *desirable,* because many applicants have language difficulties
    C. *undesirable,* because it is the inalienable right of every person to answer as he sees fit
    D. *undesirable,* because applicants may tend to agree with the answer proposed by the interviewer even when the answer is not entirely correct

1.____

2. When an initial interview is being conducted, one way of starting is to explain the purpose of the interview to the applicant. The practice of starting the interview with such an explanation is generally

    A. *desirable,* because the applicant can then understand why the interview is necessary and what will be accomplished by it
    B. *desirable,* because it creates the rapport which is necessary to successful interviewing
    C. *undesirable,* because time will be saved by starting directly with the questions which must be asked
    D. *undesirable,* because the interviewer should have the choice of starting an interview in any manner he prefers

2.____

3. For you to use responses such as "That's interesting," "Uh-huh" and "Good" during an interview with a patient is

    A. *desirable,* because they indicate that the investigator is attentive
    B. *undesirable,* because they are meaningless to the patient
    C. *desirable,* because the investigator is not supposed to talk excessively
    D. *undesirable,* because they tend to encourage the patient to speak freely

3.____

4. During the course of a routine interview, the BEST tone of voice for an interviewer to use is

    A. authoritative   B. uncertain
    C. formal   D. conversational

4.____

5. It is recommended that interviews which inquire into the personal background of an individual should be held in private. The BEST reason for this practice is that privacy

    A. allows the individual to talk freely about the details of his background
    B. induces contemplative thought on the part of the interviewed individual
    C. prevents any interruptions by departmental personnel during the interview
    D. most closely resembles the atmosphere of the individual's personal life

5.____

6. Assume that you are interviewing a patient to determine whether he has any savings accounts. To obtain this information, the MOST effective way to phrase your question would be:

    A. "You don't have any savings, do you?"
    B. "At which bank do you have a savings account?"
    C. "Do you have a savings account?"
    D. "May I assume that you have a savings account?"

6.____

7. You are interviewing a patient who is not cooperating to the extent necessary to get all required information. Therefore, you decide to be more forceful in your approach.
In this situation, such a course of action is

    A. *advisable,* because such a change in approach may help to increase the patient's participation
    B. *advisable,* because you will be using your authority more effectively
    C. *inadvisable,* because you will not be able to change this approach if it doesn't produce results
    D. *inadvisable,* because an aggressive approach generally reduces the validity of the interview

7.____

8. You have attempted to interview a patient on two separate occasions, and both attempts were unsuccessful. The patient has been totally uncooperative and you sense a personal hostility toward you.
Of the following, the BEST way to handle this type of situation would be to

    A. speak to the patient in a courteous manner and ask him to explain exactly what he dislikes about you
    B. inform the patient that you will not allow personality conflicts to disrupt the interview
    C. make no further attempt to interview the patient and recommend that he be billed in full
    D. discuss the problem with your supervisor and suggest that another investigator be assigned to try to interview the patient

8.____

9. At the beginning of an interview, a patient with normal vision tells you that he is reluctant to discuss his finances. You realize that it will be necessary in this case to ask detailed questions about his net income. When you begin this line of questioning, of the following, the LEAST important aspect you should consider is your

    A. precise wording of the question
    B. manner of questioning
    C. tone of voice
    D. facial expressions

9.____

10. A caseworker under your supervision has been assigned the task of interviewing a man who is applying for foster home placement for his two children. The caseworker seeks your advice as to how to question this man, stating that she finds the applicant to be a timid and self-conscious person who seems torn between the necessity of having to answer the worker's questions truthfully and the effect he thinks his answers will have on his application. Of the following, the BEST method for the caseworker to use in order to determine the essential facts in this case is to

10.____

A. assure the applicant that he need not worry since the majority of applications for foster home placement are approved
B. delay the applicant's narration of the facts important to the case until his embarrassment and fears have been overcome
C. ignore the statements made by the applicant and obtain all the required information from his friends and relatives
D. inform the applicant that all statements made by him will be verified and are subject to the law governing perjury

11. Assume that a worker is interviewing a boy in his assigned group in order to help him find a job. At the BEGINNING of the interview, the worker should

A. suggest a possible job for the youth
B. refer the youth to an employment agency
C. discuss the youth's work history and skills with him
D. refer the youth to the manpower and career development agency

11._____

12. As part of the investigation to locate an absent father, you make a field visit to interview one of the father's friends. Before beginning the interview, you identify yourself to the friend and show him your official identification.
For you to do this is, generally,

A. *good practice*, because the friend will have proof that you are authorized to make such confidential investigations
B. *poor practice*, because the friend may not answer your questions when he knows why you are interviewing him
C. *good practice*, because your supervisor can confirm from the friend that you actually made the interview
D. *poor practice*, because the friend may warn the absent father that your agency is looking for him

12._____

13. You are interviewing a client in his home as part of your investigation of an anonymous complaint that he has been receiving Medicaid fraudulently. During the interview, the client frequently interrupts your questions to discuss the hardships of his life and the bitterness he feels about his medical condition.
Of the following, the BEST way for you to deal with these discussions is to

A. cut them off abruptly, since the client is probably just trying to avoid answering your questions
B. listen patiently, since these discussions may be helpful to the client and may give you information for your investigation
C. remind the client that you are investigating a complaint against him and he must answer directly
D. seek to gain the client's confidence by discussing any personal or medical problems which you yourself may have

13._____

14. While interviewing an absent father to determine his ability to pay child support, you realize that his answers to some of your questions contradict his answers to other questions.
Of the following, the BEST way for you to try to get accurate information from the father is to

A. confront him with his contradictory answers and demand an explanation from him

14._____

B. use your best judgment as to which of his answers are accurate and question him accordingly
C. tell him that he has misunderstood your questions and that he must clarify his answers
D. ask him the same questions in different words and follow up his answers with related questions

15. Assume that an applicant, obviously under a great deal of stress, talks continuously and rambles, making it difficult for you to determine the exact problem and her need. In order to make the interview more successful, it would be BEST for you to   15.____

A. interrupt the applicant and ask her specific questions in order to get the information you need
B. tell the applicant that her rambling may be a basic cause of her problem
C. let the applicant continue talking as long as she wishes
D. ask the applicant to get to the point because other people are waiting for you

16. A worker must be able to interview clients all day and still be able to listen and maintain interest.   16.____
Of the following, it is MOST important for you to show interest in the client because, if you appear interested,

A. the client is more likely to appreciate your professional status
B. the client is more likely to disclose a greater amount of information
C. the client is less likely to tell lies
D. you are more likely to gain your supervisor's approval

17. When you are interviewing clients, it is important to notice and record how they say what they say—angrily, nervously, or with "body English"—because these signs may   17.____

A. tell you that the client's words are the opposite of what the client feels and you may need to dig to find out what those feelings are
B. be the prelude to violent behavior which no aide is prepared to handle
C. show that the client does not really deserve serious consideration
D. be important later should you be asked to defend what you did for the client

18. The patient you are interviewing is reticent and guarded in responding to your questions. He is not providing the information needed to complete his application for medical assistance.   18.____
In this situation, the one of the following which is the most appropriate course of action for you to take FIRST is to

A. end the interview and ask him to contact you when he is ready to answer your questions
B. advise the patient that you cannot end the interview until he has provided all the information you need to complete the application
C. emphasize to the patient the importance of the questions and the need to answer them in order to complete the application
D. advise the patient that if he answers your questions the interview will be easier for both of you

19. At the end of an interview with a patient, he describes a problem he is having with his teenage son, who is often truant and may be using narcotics. The patient asks you for advice in handling his son.
Of the following, the MOST appropriate action for you to take is to

    A. make an appointment to see the patient and his son together
    B. give the patient a list of drug counseling programs to which he may refer his son
    C. suggest to the patient that his immediate concern should be his own hospitalization rather than his son's problem
    D. tell the patient that you are not qualified to assist him but will attempt to find out who can

19.____

20. A MOST appropriate condition in the use of direct questions to obtain personal data in an interview is that, whenever possible,

    A. the direct questions be used only as a means of encouraging the person interviewed to talk about himself
    B. provision be made for recording the information
    C. the direct questions be used only after all other methods have failed
    D. the person being interviewed understands the reason for requesting the information

20.____

KEY (CORRECT ANSWERS)

1.	D	11.	C
2.	A	12.	A
3.	A	13.	B
4.	D	14.	D
5.	A	15.	A
6.	B	16.	B
7.	A	17.	A
8.	D	18.	C
9.	A	19.	D
10.	B	20.	D

PREPARING WRITTEN MATERIAL

PARAGRAPH REARRANGEMENT
COMMENTARY

The sentences which follow are in scrambled order. You are to rearrange them in proper order and indicate the letter choice containing the correct answer at the space at the right.

Each group of sentences in this section is actually a paragraph presented in scrambled order. Each sentence in the group has a place in that paragraph; no sentence is to be left out. You are to read each group of sentences and decide upon the best order in which to put the sentences so as to form as well-organized paragraph.

The questions in this section measure the ability to solve a problem when all the facts relevant to its solution are not given.

More specifically, certain positions of responsibility and authority require the employee to discover connections between events sometimes, apparently, unrelated. In order to do this, the employee will find it necessary to correctly infer that unspecified events have probably occurred or are likely to occur. This ability becomes especially important when action must be taken on incomplete information.

Accordingly, these questions require competitors to choose among several suggested alternatives, each of which presents a different sequential arrangement of the events. Competitors must choose the MOST logical of the suggested sequences.

In order to do so, they may be required to draw on general knowledge to infer missing concepts or events that are essential to sequencing the given events. Competitors should be careful to infer only what is essential to the sequence. The plausibility of the wrong alternatives will always require the inclusion of unlikely events or of additional chains of events which are NOT essential to sequencing the given events.

It's very important to remember that you are looking for the best of the four possible choices, and that the best choice of all may not even be one of the answers you're given to choose from.

There is no one right way to solve these problems. Many people have found it helpful to first write out the order of the sentences, as they would have arranged them, on their scrap paper before looking at the possible answers. If their optimum answer is there, this can save them some time. If it isn't, this method can still give insight into solving the problem. Others find it most helpful to just go through each of the possible choices, contrasting each as they go along. You should use whatever method feels comfortable, and works, for you.

While most of these types of questions are not that difficult, we've added a higher percentage of the difficult type, just to give you more practice. Usually there are only one or two questions on this section that contain such subtle distinctions that you're unable to answer confidently, and you then may find yourself stuck deciding between two possible choices, neither of which you're sure about.

———

EXAMINATION SECTION
TEST 1

DIRECTIONS: Each question consists of several sentences which can be arranged in a logical sequence. For each question, select the choice which places the numbered sentences in the MOST logical sequence. *PRINT THE LETTER OF
THE CORRECT ANSWER IN THE SPACE AT THE RIGHT.*

1. I.   A body was found in the woods.   1.____
    II. A man proclaimed innocence.
    III. The owner of a gun was located.
    IV. A gun was traced.
    V.   The owner of a gun was questioned.
    The CORRECT answer is:

    A. IV, III, V, II, I   B. II, I, IV, III, V
    C. I, IV, III, V, II   D. I, III, V, II, IV
    E. I, II, IV, III, V

2. I.   A man was in a hunting accident.   2.____
    II. A man fell down a flight of steps.
    III. A man lost his vision in one eye.
    IV. A man broke his leg.
    V.   A man had to walk with a cane.
    The CORRECT answer is:

    A. II, IV, V, I, III   B. IV, V, I, III, II
    C. III, I, IV, V, II   D. I, III, V, II, IV
    E. I, III, II, IV, V

3. I.   A man is offered a new job.   3.____
    II. A woman is offered a new job.
    III. A man works as a waiter.
    IV. A woman works as a waitress.
    V.   A woman gives notice.
    The CORRECT answer is:

    A. IV, II, V, III, I   B. IV, II, V, I, III
    C. II, IV, V, III, I   D. III, I, IV, II, V
    E. IV, III, II, V, I

4. I.   A train left the station late.   4.____
    II. A man was late for work.
    III. A man lost his job.
    IV. Many people complained because the train was late.
    V.   There was a traffic jam.
    The CORRECT answer is:

    A. V, II, I, IV, III   B. V, I, IV, II, III
    C. V, I, II, IV, III   D. I, V, IV, II, III
    E. II, I, IV, V, III

5.   I.   The burden of proof as to each issue is determined before trial and remains upon the same party throughout the trial.
     II. The jury is at liberty to believe one witness' testimony as against a number of contradictory witnesses.
     III. In a civil case, the party bearing the burden of proof is required to prove his contention by a fair preponderance of the evidence.
     IV. However, it must be noted that a fair preponderance of evidence does not necessarily mean a greater number of witnesses.
     V.   The burden of proof is the burden which rests upon one of the parties to an action to persuade the trier of the facts, generally the jury, that a proposition he asserts is true.
     VI. If the evidence is equally balanced, or if it leaves the jury in such doubt as to be unable to decide the controversy either way, judgment must be given against the party upon whom the burden of proof rests.

The CORRECT answer is:

A.   III, II, V, IV, I, VI   B.   I, II, VI, V, III, IV
C.   III, IV, V, I, II, VI   D.   V, I, III, VI, IV, II
E.   I, V, III, VI, IV, II

5.____

6.   I.   If a parent is without assets and is unemployed, he cannot be convicted of the crime of non-support of a child.
     II. The term *sufficient ability* has been held to mean sufficient financial ability.
     III. It does not matter if his unemployment is by choice or unavoidable circumstances.
     IV. If he fails to take any steps at all, he may be liable to prosecution for endangering the welfare of a child.
     V.   Under the penal law, a parent is responsible for the support of his minor child only if the parent is of *sufficient ability*.
     VI. An indigent parent may meet his obligation by borrowing money or by seeking aid under the provisions of the Social Welfare Law.

The CORRECT answer is:

A.   VI, I, V, III, II, IV   B.   I, III, V, II, IV, VI
C.   V, II, I, III, VI, IV   D.   I, VI, IV, V, II, III
E.   II, V, I, III, VI, IV

6.____

7.   I.   Consider, for example, the case of a rabble rouser who urges a group of twenty people to go out and break the windows of a nearby factory.
     II. Therefore, the law fills the indicated gap with the crime of *inciting to riot*.
     III. A person is considered guilty of inciting to riot when he urges ten or more persons to engage in tumultuous and violent conduct of a kind likely to create public alarm.
     IV. However, if he has not obtained the cooperation of at least four people, he cannot be charged with unlawful assembly.
     V.   The charge of inciting to riot was added to the law to cover types of conduct which cannot be classified as either the crime of *riot* or the crime of *unlawful assembly*.
     VI. If he acquires the acquiescence of at least four of them, he is guilty of unlawful assembly even if the project does not materialize.

The CORRECT answer is:

7.____

A. III, V, I, VI, IV, II
C. III, IV, I, V, II, VI
E. V, III, I, VI, IV, II
B. V, I, IV, VI, II, III
D. V, I, IV, VI, III, II

8.　I. If, however, the rebuttal evidence presents an issue of credibility, it is for the jury to determine whether the presumption has, in fact, been destroyed.　8.____

II. Once sufficient evidence to the contrary is introduced, the presumption disappears from the trial.

III. The effect of a presumption is to place the burden upon the adversary to come forward with evidence to rebut the presumption.

IV. When a presumption is overcome and ceases to exist in the case, the fact or facts which gave rise to the presumption still remain.

V. Whether a presumption has been overcome is ordinarily a question for the court.

VI. Such information may furnish a basis for a logical inference.

The CORRECT answer is:

A. IV, VI, II, V, I, III
C. V, III, VI, IV, II, I
E. II, III, V, I, IV, VI
B. III, II, V, I, IV, VI
D. V, IV, I, II, VI, III

9.　I. An executive may answer a letter by writing his reply on the face of the letter itself instead of having a return letter typed.　9.____

II. This procedure is efficient because it saves the executive's time, the typist's time, and saves office file space.

III. Copying machines are used in small offices as well as large offices to save time and money in making brief replies to business letters.

IV. A copy is made on a copying machine to go into the company files, while the original is mailed back to the sender.

The CORRECT answer is:

A. I, II, IV, III
C. III, I, IV, II
B. I, IV, II, III
D. III, IV, II, I

10.　I. Most organizations favor one of the types but always include the others to a lesser degree.　10.____

II. However, we can detect a definite trend toward greater use of symbolic control.

III. We suggest that our local police agencies are today primarily utilizing material control.

IV. Control can be classified into three types: physical, material, and symbolic.

The CORRECT answer is:

A. IV, II, III, I
C. III, IV, II, I
B. II, I, IV, III
D. IV, I, III, II

11.　I. Project residents had first claim to this use, followed by surrounding neighborhood children.　11.____

II. By contrast, recreation space within the project's interior was found to be used more often by both groups.

III. Studies of the use of project grounds in many cities showed grounds left open for public use were neglected and unused, both by residents and by members of the surrounding community.

IV. Project residents had clearly laid claim to the play spaces, setting up and enforcing unwritten rules for use.

V. Each group, by experience, found their activities easily disrupted by other groups, and their claim to the use of space for recreation difficult to enforce.

The CORRECT answer is:

A. IV, V, I, II, III
B. V, II, IV, III, I
C. I, IV, III, II, V
D. III, V, II, IV, I

12. I. They do not consider the problems correctable within the existing subsidy formula and social policy of accepting all eligible applicants regardless of social behavior and lifestyle.

II. A recent survey, however, indicated that tenants believe these problems correctable by local housing authorities and management within the existing financial formula.

III. Many of the problems and complaints concerning public housing management and design have created resentment between the tenant and the landlord.

IV. This same survey indicated that administrators and managers do not agree with the tenants.

The CORRECT answer is:

A. II, I, III, IV
B. I, III, IV, II
C. III, II, IV, I
D. IV, II, I, III

12._____

13. I. In single-family residences, there is usually enough distance between tenants to prevent occupants from annoying one another.

II. For example, a certain small percentage of tenant families has one or more members addicted to alcohol.

III. While managers believe in the right of individuals to live as they choose, the manager becomes concerned when the pattern of living jeopardizes others' rights.

IV. Still others turn night into day, staging lusty entertainments which carry on into the hours when most tenants are trying to sleep.

V. In apartment buildings, however, tenants live so closely together that any misbehavior can result in unpleasant living conditions.

VI. Other families engage in violent argument.

The CORRECT answer is:

A. III, II, V, IV, VI, I
B. I, V, II, VI, IV, III
C. II, V, IV, I, III, VI
D. IV, II, V, VI, III, I

13._____

14. I. Congress made the commitment explicit in the Housing Act of 1949, establishing as a national goal the realization of *a decent home and suitable environment for every American family.*

II. The result has been that the goal of decent home and suitable environment is still as far distant as ever for the disadvantaged urban family.

III. In spite of this action by Congress, federal housing programs have continued to be fragmented and grossly underfunded.

IV. The passage of the National Housing Act signalled a new federal commitment to provide housing for the nation's citizens.

The CORRECT answer is:

A. I, IV, III, II
B. IV, I, III, II
C. IV, I, II, III
D. II, IV, I, III

14._____

15.   I.   The greater expense does not necessarily involve *exploitation*, but it is often per-   15.____
ceived as exploitative and unfair by those who are aware of the price differences
involved, but unaware of operating costs.

II.   Ghetto residents believe they are *exploited* by local merchants, and evidence
substantiates some of these beliefs.

III.   However, stores in low-income areas were more likely to be small independents,
which could not achieve the economies available to supermarket chains and
were, therefore, more likely to charge higher prices, and the customers were
more likely to buy smaller-sized packages which are more expensive per unit of
measure.

IV.   A study conducted in one city showed that distinctly higher prices were charged
for goods sold in ghetto stores than in other areas.

The CORRECT answer is:

A.   IV, II, I, III   B.   IV, I, III, II
C.   II, IV, III, I   D.   II, III, IV, I

KEY (CORRECT ANSWERS)

1.	C		6.	C
2.	E		7.	A
3.	B		8.	B
4.	B		9.	C
5.	D		10.	D

11.	D
12.	C
13.	B
14.	B
15.	C

PREPARING WRITTEN MATERIALS

EXAMINATION SECTION
TEST 1

DIRECTIONS: Each question contains a sentence. Read each sentence carefully to decide whether it is correct. Then, in the space at the right, mark your answer:
- A. If the sentence is incorrect because of bad grammar or sentence structure;
- B. If the sentence is incorrect because of bad punctuation;
- C. If the sentence is incorrect because of bad capitalization;
- D. If the sentence is correct.

Each incorrect sentence has only one type of error. Consider a sentence correct if it has no errors, although there may be other correct ways of saying the same thing.

SAMPLE QUESTION I; One of our clerks were promoted yesterday.

The subject of this sentence is *one,* so the verb should be *was promoted* instead of *were promoted.* Since the sentence is incorrect because of bad grammar, the answer to Sample Question I is A.

SAMPLE QUESTION II: Between you and me, I would prefer not going there.

Since this sentence is correct, the answer to Sample Question II is D.

1. The National alliance of Businessmen is trying to persuade private businesses to hire youth in the summertime.   1._____

2. The supervisor who is on vacation, is in charge of processing vouchers.   2._____

3. The activity of the committee at its conferences is always stimulating.   3._____

4. After checking the addresses again, the letters went to the mailroom.   4._____

5. The director, as well as the employees, are interested in sharing the dividends. 5._____

6. The experiments conducted by professor Alford were described at a recent meeting of our organization.   6._____

7. I shall be glad to discuss these matters with whoever represents the Municipal Credit Union.   7._____

8. In my opinion, neither Mr. Price nor Mr. Roth knows how to operate this office appliance. 8._____

9. The supervisor, as well as the other stenographers, were unable to transcribe Miss Johnson's shorthand notes.   9._____

10. Important functions such as, recruiting and training, are performed by our unit. 10._____

11. Realizing that many students are interested in this position, we sent announcements to all the High Schools.   11.____

12. After pointing out certain incorrect conclusions, the report was revised by Mr. Clark and submitted to Mr. Batson.   12.____

13. The employer contributed two hundred dollars; the employees, one hundred dollars.   13.____

14. He realized that the time, when a supervisor could hire and fire, was over.   14.____

15. The complaints received by Commissioner Regan was the cause of the change in policy.   15.____

16. Any report, that is to be sent to the Federal Security Administration, must be approved and signed by Mr. Yound.   16.____

17. Of the two stenographers, Miss Rand is the more accurate.   17.____

18. Since the golf courses are crowded during the Summer, more men are needed to maintain the courses in good playing condition.   18.____

19. Although he invited Mr. Frankel and I to attend a meeting of the Civil Service Assembly, we were unable to accept his invitation.   19.____

20. Only the employees who worked overtime last week may leave one hour earlier today.   20.____

21. We need someone who can speak french fluently.   21.____

22. A tall, elderly, man entered the office and asked to see Mr. Brown.   22.____

23. The clerk insisted that he had filed the correspondence in the proper cabinet.   23.____

24. "Will you assist us," he asked?   24.____

25. According to the information contained in the report, a large quantity of paper and envelopes were used by this bureau last year.   25.____

KEY (CORRECT ANSWERS)

1.	C	11.	C
2.	B	12.	A
3.	D	13.	D
4.	A	14.	B
5.	A	15.	A
6.	C	16.	B
7.	D	17.	D
8.	D	18.	C
9.	A	19.	A
10.	B	20.	D

21.	C
22.	B
23.	D
24.	B
25.	A

———

TEST 2

DIRECTIONS: Each question consists of a sentence which may be classified appropriately under one of the following four categories:
    A. Incorrect because of faulty grammar or sentence structure;
    B. Incorrect because of faulty punctuation;
    C. Incorrect because of faulty capitalization;
    D. Correct

Examine each sentence carefully. Then, in the space at the right, print the capital letter preceding the option which is the BEST of the four suggested above. All incorrect sentences contain only one type of error. Consider a sentence correct if it contains none of the types of errors mentioned, although there may be other correct ways of expressing the same thought.

1. Mrs. Black the supervisor of the unit, has many important duties.   1._____

2. We spoke to the man whom you saw yesterday.   2._____

3. When a holiday falls on Sunday, it is officially celebrated on monday.   3._____

4. Of the two reports submitted, this one is the best.   4._____

5. Each staff member, including the accountants, were invited to the meeting.   5._____

6. Give the package to whomever calls for it.   6._____

7. To plan the work is our responsibility; to carry it out is his.   7._____

8. "May I see the person in charge of this office," asked the visitor?   8._____

9. He knows that it was not us who prepared the report.   9._____

10. These problems were brought to the attention of senator Johnson.   10._____

11. The librarian classifies all books periodicals and documents.   11._____

12. Any employee who uses an adding machine realizes its importance.   12._____

13. Instead of coming to the office, the clerk should of come to the supply room.   13._____

14. He asked, "will your staff assist us?"   14._____

15. Having been posted on the bulletin board, we were certain that the announcements would be read.   15._____

16. He was not informed, that he would have to work overtime.   16._____

17. The wind blew several papers off of his desk.   17._____

18. Charles Dole, who is a member of the committee, was asked to confer with commissioner Wilson.   18._____

19. Miss Bell will issue a copy to whomever asks for one.   19._____

20. Most employees, and he is no exception do not like to work overtime. 20._____

21. This is the man whom you interviewed last week. 21._____

22. Of the two cities visited, White Plains is the cleanest. 22._____

23. Although he was willing to work on other holidays, he refused to work on Labor day. 23._____

24. If an employee wishes to attend the conference, he should fill out the necessary forms. 24._____

25. The division chief reports that an engineer and an inspector is needed for this special survey. 25._____

_____

KEY (CORRECT ANSWERS)

1.	B		11.	B
2.	D		12.	D
3.	C		13.	A
4.	A		14.	C
5.	A		15.	A
6.	A		16.	B
7.	D		17.	A
8.	B		18.	C
9.	A		19.	A
10.	C		20.	B

21.	D
22.	A
23.	C
24.	D
25.	A

_____

TEST 3

DIRECTIONS: Each question consists of a sentence which may be classified appropriately under one of the following four categories:
- A. Incorrect because of faulty grammar or sentence structure;
- B. Incorrect because of faulty punctuation;
- C. Incorrect because of faulty capitalization;
- D. Correct

Examine each sentence carefully. Then, in the space at the right, indicate the letter preceding the category which is the BEST of the four suggested above. Each incorrect sentence contains only one type of error. Consider a sentence correct if it contains none of the types of errors mentioned, although there may be other correct ways of expressing the same thought.

1. We have learned that there was more than twelve people present at the meeting. 1.____

2. Every one of the employees is able to do this kind of work. 2.____

3. Neither the supervisor nor his assistant are in the office today. 3.____

4. The office manager announced that any clerk, who volunteered for the assignment, would be rewarded. 4.____

5. After looking carefully in all the files, the letter was finally found on a desk. 5.____

6. In answer to the clerk's question, the supervisor said, "this assignment must be completed today." 6.____

7. The office manager says that he can permit only you and me to go to the meeting. 7.____

8. The supervisor refused to state who he would assign to the reception unit. 8.____

9. At the last meeting, he said that he would interview us in September. 9.____

10. Mr. Jones, who is one of our most experienced employees has been placed in charge of the main office. 10.____

11. I think that this adding machine is the most useful of the two we have in our office. 11.____

12. Between you and I, our new stenographer is not as competent as our former stenographer. 12.____

13. The new assignment should be given to whoever can do the work rapidly. 13.____

14. Mrs. Smith, as well as three other typists, was assigned to the new office. 14.____

15. The staff assembled for the conference on time but, the main speaker arrived late. 15.____

16. The work was assigned to Miss Green and me. 16.____

17. The staff regulations state that an employee, who is frequently tardy, may receive a negative evaluation. 17.____

18. He is the kind of person who is always willing to undertake difficult assignments. 18.____

144

19. Mr. Wright's request cannot be granted under no conditions.   19.____

20. George Colt a new employee, was asked to deliver the report to the Domestic Relations Court.   20.____

21. The supervisor entered the room and said, "The work must be completed today."   21.____

22. The employees were given their assignments and, they were asked to begin work immediately.   22.____

23. The letter will be sent to the United States senate this week.   23.____

24. When the supervisor entered the room, he noticed that the book was laying on the desk.   24.____

25. The price of the pens were higher than the price of the pencils.   25.____

KEY (CORRECT ANSWERS)

1.	A	11.	A
2.	D	12.	A
3.	A	13.	D
4.	B	14.	D
5.	A	15.	B
6.	C	16.	D
7.	D	17.	B
8.	A	18.	D
9.	C	19.	A
10.	B	20.	B

21.	D
22.	B
23.	C
24.	A
25.	A

---

EXAMINATION SECTION
TEST 1

DIRECTIONS: Each question or incomplete statement is followed by several suggested answers or completions. Select the one that BEST answers the question or completes the statement. *PRINT THE LETTER OF THE CORRECT ANSWER IN THE SPACE AT THE RIGHT.*

1. Which of the following sentences is punctuated INCORRECTLY?   1.____

    A. Johnson said, "One tiny virus, Blanche, can multiply so fast that it will become 200 viruses in 25 minutes."
    B. With economic pressures hitting them from all sides, American farmers have become the weak link in the food chain.
    C. The degree to which this is true, of course, depends on the personalities of the people involved, the subject matter, and the atmosphere in general.
    D. "What loneliness, asked George Eliot, is more lonely than distrust?"

2. Which of the following sentences is punctuated INCORRECTLY?   2.____

    A. Based on past experiences, do you expect the plumber to show up late, not have the right parts, and overcharge you.
    B. When polled, however, the participants were most concerned that it be convenient.
    C. No one mentioned the flavor of the coffee, and no one seemed to care that china was used instead of plastic.
    D. As we said before, sometimes people view others as things; they don't see them as living, breathing beings like themselves.

3. Convention members travelled here from Kingston New York Pittsfield Massachusetts Bennington Vermont and Hartford Connecticut.   3.____
How many commas should there be in the above sentence?

    A. 3   B. 4   C. 5   D. 6

4. Of the two speakers the one who spoke about human rights is more famous and more humble.   4.____
How many commas should there be in the above sentence?

    A. 1   B. 2   C. 3   D. 4

5. Which sentence is punctuated INCORRECTLY?   5.____

    A. Five people voted no; two voted yes; one person abstained.
    B. Well, consider what has been said here today, but we won't make any promises.
    C. Anthropologists divide history into three major periods: the Stone Age, the Bronze Age, and the Iron Age.
    D. Therefore, we may create a stereotype about people who are unsuccessful; we may see them as lazy, unintelligent, or afraid of success.

6. Which sentence is punctuated INCORRECTLY?   6.____

    A. Studies have found that the unpredictability of customer behavior can lead to a great deal of stress, particularly if the behavior is unpleasant or if the employee has little control over it.

B. If this degree of emotion and variation can occur in spectator sports, imagine the role that perceptions can play when there are <u>real</u> stakes involved.
C. At other times, however hidden expectations may sabotage or severely damage an encounter without anyone knowing what happened.
D. There are usually four issues to look for in a conflict: differences in values, goals, methods, and facts.

Questions 7-10.

DIRECTIONS: Questions 7 through 10 test your ability to distinguish between words that sound alike but are spelled differently and have different meanings. In the following groups of sentences, one of the underlined words is used incorrectly.

7. A. By <u>accepting</u> responsibility for their actions, managers promote trust.   7.____
    B. Dropping hints or making <u>illusions</u> to things that you would like changed sometimes leads to resentment.
    C. The entire unit <u>loses</u> respect for the manager and resents the reprimand.
    D. Many people are <u>averse</u> to confronting problems directly; they would rather avoid them.

8. A. What does this say about the <u>effect</u> our expectations have on those we supervise?   8.____
    B. In an effort to save time between 9 A.M. and 1 P.M., the staff members devised <u>their</u> own interpretation of what was to be done on these forms.
    C. The task master's <u>principal</u> concern is for getting the work done; he or she is not concerned about the needs or interests of employees.
    D. The advisor's main objective was increasing Angela's ability to invest her <u>capitol</u> wisely.

9. A. A typical problem is that people have to cope with the internal <u>censer</u> of their feelings.   9.____
    B. Sometimes, in their attempt to sound more learned, people speak in ways that are barely <u>comprehensible</u>.
    C. The <u>council</u> will meet next Friday to decide whether Abrams should continue as representative.
    D. His <u>descent</u> from grace was assured by that final word.

10. A. The doctor said that John's leg had to remain <u>stationary</u> or it would not heal properly.   10.____
    B. There is a city <u>ordinance</u> against parking too close to fire hydrants.
    C. Meyer's problem is that he is never <u>discrete</u> when talking about office politics.
    D. Mrs. Thatcher probably worked harder <u>than</u> any other British Prime Minister had ever worked.

Questions 11-20.

DIRECTIONS: For each of the following groups of sentences in Questions 11 through 20, select the sentence which is the BEST example of English usage and grammar.

11.   A. She is a woman who, at age sixty, is distinctly attractive and cares about how they look.   11.____
       B. It was a seemingly impossible search, and no one knew the problems better than she.
       C. On the surface, they are all sweetness and light, but his morbid character is under it.
       D. The minicopier, designed to appeal to those who do business on the run like architects in the field or business travelers, weigh about four pounds.

12.   A. Neither the administrators nor the union representative regret the decision to settle the disagreement.   12.____
       B. The plans which are made earlier this year were no longer being considered.
       C. I would have rode with him if I had known he was leaving at five.
       D. I don't know who she said had it.

13.   A. Writing at a desk, the memo was handed to her for immediate attention.   13.____
       B. Carla didn't water Carl's plants this week, which she never does.
       C. Not only are they good workers, with excellent writing and speaking skills, and they get to the crux of any problem we hand them.
       D. We've noticed that this enthusiasm for undertaking new projects sometimes interferes with his attention to detail.

14.   A. It's obvious that Nick offends people by being unruly, inattentive, and having no patience.   14.____
       B. Marcia told Genie that she would have to leave soon.
       C. Here are the papers you need to complete your investigation.
       D. Julio was startled by you're comment.

15.   A. The new manager has done good since receiving her promotion, but her secretary has helped her a great deal.   15.____
       B. One of the personnel managers approached John and tells him that the client arrived unexpectedly.
       C. If somebody can supply us with the correct figures, they should do so immediately.
       D. Like zealots, advocates seek power because they want to influence the policies and actions of an organization.

16.   A. Between you and me, Chris probably won't finish this assignment in time.   16.____
       B. Rounding the corner, the snack bar appeared before us.
       C. Parker's radical reputation made to the Supreme Court his appointment impossible.
       D. By the time we arrived, Marion finishes briefing James and returns to Hank's office.

17. A. As we pointed out earlier, the critical determinant of the success of middle manag-   17.____
          ers is their ability to communicate well with others.
     B. The lecturer stated there wasn't no reason for bad supervision.
     C. We are well aware whose at fault in this instance.
     D. When planning important changes, it's often wise to seek the partic-
          ipation of others because employees often have much valuable
          ideas to offer.

18. A. Joan had ought to throw out those old things that were damaged when the roof   18.____
          leaked.
     B. I spose he'll let us know what he's decided when he finally comes to
          a decision.
     C. Carmen was walking to work when she suddenly realized that she
          had left her lunch on the table as she passed the market.
     D. Are these enough plants for your new office?

19. A. First move the lever forward, and then they should lift the ribbon casing before try-   19.____
          ing to take it out.
     B. Michael finished quickest than any other person in the office.
     C. There is a special meeting for we committee members today at 4
          p.m.
     D. My husband is worried about our having to work overtime next
          week.

20. A. Another source of conflicts are individuals who possess very poor interpersonal   20.____
          skills.
     B. It is difficult for us to work with him on projects because these kinds
          of people are not interested in team building.
     C. Each of the departments was represented at the meeting.
     D. Poor boy, he never should of past that truck on the right.

Questions 21-28.

DIRECTIONS: In Questions 21 through 28, there may be a problem with English grammar or
             usage. If a problem does exist, select the letter that indicates the most effec-
             tive change. If no problem exists, select choice A.

21. He rushed her to the hospital and stayed with her, even though this took quite a bit of his   21.____
     time, he didn't charge her anything.

     A. No changes are necessary
     B. Change even though to although
     C. Change the first comma to a period and capitalize even
     D. Change rushed to had rushed

22. Waiting that appears unfairly feels longer than waiting that seems justified.   22.____

     A. No changes are necessary
     B. Change unfairly to unfair
     C. Change appears to seems
     D. Change longer to longest

23. May be you and the person who argued with you will be able to reach an agreement.   23.____

    A. No changes are necessary
    B. Change will be to <u>were</u>
    C. Change <u>argued with</u> to <u>had an argument with</u>
    D. Change <u>May be</u> to <u>Maybe</u>

24. Any one of them could of taken the file while you were having coffee.   24.____

    A. No changes are necessary
    B. Change <u>any one</u> to <u>anyone</u>
    C. Change <u>of</u> to <u>have</u>
    D. Change <u>were having</u> to <u>were out having</u>

25. While people get jobs or move from poverty level to better paying employment, they stop   25.____
receiving benefits and start paying taxes.

    A. No changes are necessary
    B. Change <u>While</u> to <u>As</u>
    C. Change <u>stop</u> to <u>will stop</u>
    D. Change <u>get</u> to <u>obtain</u>

26. Maribeth's phone rang while talking to George about the possibility of their meeting Tom   26.____
at three this afternoon.

    A. No changes are necessary
    B. Change <u>their</u> to <u>her</u>
    C. Move <u>to George</u> so that it follows <u>Tom</u>
    D. Change <u>talking</u> to <u>she was talking</u>

27. According to their father, Lisa is smarter than Chris, but Emily is the smartest of the three   27.____
sisters.

    A. No changes are necessary
    B. Change <u>their</u> to <u>her</u>
    C. Change <u>is</u> to <u>was</u>
    D. Make two sentences, changing the second comma to a period and omitting <u>but</u>

28. Yesterday, Mark and he claim that Carl took Carol's ideas and used them inappropriately.   28.____

    A. No changes are necessary
    B. Change <u>claim</u> to <u>claimed</u>
    C. Change <u>inappropriately</u> to <u>inappropriate</u>
    D. Change <u>Carol's</u> to <u>Carols'</u>

Questions 29-34.

DIRECTIONS: For each group of sentences in Questions 29 through 34, select the choice
that represents the BEST editing of the problem sentence.

29. The managers expected employees to be at their desks at all times, but they would   29.____
always be late or leave unannounced.

A. The managers wanted employees to always be at their desks, but they would always be late or leave unannounced.
B. Although the managers expected employees to be at their desks no matter what came up, they would always be late and leave without telling anyone.
C. Although the managers expected employees to be at their desks at all times, the managers would always be late or leave without telling anyone.
D. The managers expected the employee to never leave their desks, but they would always be late or leave without telling anyone.

30. The one who is department manager he will call you to discuss the problem tomorrow morning at 10 A.M.   30.____

   A. The one who is department manager will call you tomorrow morning at ten to discuss the problem.
   B. The department manager will call you to discuss the problem tomorrow at 10 A.M.
   C. Tomorrow morning at 10 A.M., the department manager will call you to discuss the problem.
   D. Tomorrow morning the department manager will call you to discuss the problem.

31. A conference on child care in the workplace the $200 cost of which to attend may be pro-   31.____
hibitive to childcare workers who earn less than that weekly.

   A. A conference on child care in the workplace that costs $200 may be too expensive for childcare workers who earn less than that each week.
   B. A conference on child care in the workplace, the cost of which to attend is $200, may be prohibitive to childcare workers who earn less than that weekly.
   C. A conference on child care in the workplace who costs $200 may be too expensive for childcare workers who earn less than that a week.
   D. A conference on child care in the workplace which costs $200 may be too expensive to childcare workers who earn less than that on a weekly basis.

32. In accordance with estimates recently made, there are 40,000 to 50,000 nuclear weap-   32.____
ons in our world today.

   A. Because of estimates recently, there are 40,000 to 50,000 nuclear weapons in the world today.
   B. In accordance with estimates made recently, there are 40,000 to 50,000 nuclear weapons in the world today.
   C. According to estimates made recently, there are 40,000 to 50,000 weapons in the world today.
   D. According to recent estimates, there are 40,000 to 50,000 nuclear weapons in the world today.

33. Motivation is important in problem solving, but they say that excessive motivation can   33.____
inhibit the creative process.

   A. Motivation is important in problem solving, but, as they say, too much of it can inhibit the creative process.
   B. Motivation is important in problem solving and excessive motivation will inhibit the creative process.
   C. Motivation is important in problem solving, but excessive motivation can inhibit the creative process.

D. Motivation is important in problem solving because excessive motivation can inhibit the creative process.

34. In selecting the best option calls for consulting with all the people that are involved in it.　34.____

    A. In selecting the best option consulting with all the people concerned with it.
    B. Calling for the best option, we consulted all the affected people.
    C. We called all the people involved to select the best option.
    D. To be sure of selecting the best option, one should consult all the people involved.

35. There are a number of problems with the following letter. From the options below, select the version that is MOST in accordance with standard business style, tone, and form.　35.____

Dear Sir:

We are so sorry that we have had to backorder your order for 15,000 widgets and 2,300 whatzits for such a long time. We have been having incredibly bad luck lately. When your order first came in no one could get to it because my secretary was out with the flu and her replacement didn't know what she was doing, then there was the dock strike in Cucamonga which held things up for awhile, and then it just somehow got lost. We think it may have fallen behind the radiator.

We are happy to say that all these problems have been taken care of, we are caught up on supplies, and we should have the stuff to you soon, in the near future --about two weeks. You may not believe us after everything you've been through with us, but it's true.

We'll let you know as soon as we have a secure date for delivery. Thank you so much for continuing to do business with us after all the problems this probably has caused you.

Yours very sincerely,

Rob Barker

    A. Dear Sir:

       We are so sorry that we have had to backorder your order for 15,000 widgets and 2,300 whatzits. We have been having problems with staff lately and the dock strike hasn't helped anything.

       We are happy to say that all these problems have been taken care of. I've told my secretary to get right on it, and we should have the stuff to you soon. Thank you so much for continuing to do business with us after all the problems this must have caused you.

       We'll let you know as soon as we have a secure date for delivery.

       Sincerely,

       Rob Barker

B.   Dear Sir:

We regret that we haven't been able to fill your order for 15,000 widgets and 2,300 whatzits in a timely fashion.

We'll let you know as soon as we have a secure date for delivery.

Sincerely,

Rob Barker

C.   Dear Sir:

We are so very sorry that we haven't been able to fill your order for 15,000 widgets and 2,300 whatzits. We have been having incredibly bad luck lately, but things are much better now.

Thank you so much for bearing with us through all of this. We'll let you know as soon as we have a secure date for delivery.

Sincerely,

Rob Barker

D.   Dear Sir:

We are very sorry that we haven't been able to fill your order for 15,000 widgets and 2,300 whatzits. Due to unforeseen difficulties, we have had to back-order your request. At this time, supplies have caught up to demand, and we foresee a delivery date within the next two weeks.

We'll let you know as soon as we have a secure date for delivery. Thank you for your patience.

Sincerely,

Rob Barker

KEY (CORRECT ANSWERS)

1.	D		16.	A
2.	A		17.	A
3.	B		18.	D
4.	A		19.	D
5.	B		20.	C
6.	C		21.	C
7.	B		22.	B
8.	D		23.	D
9.	A		24.	C
10.	C		25.	B
11.	B		26.	D
12.	D		27.	A
13.	D		28.	B
14.	C		29.	C
15.	D		30.	B

31.	A
32.	D
33.	C
34.	D
35.	D

ARITHMETICAL REASONING
EXAMINATION SECTION
TEST 1

DIRECTIONS: Each question or incomplete statement is followed by several suggested answers or completions. Select the one that BEST answers the question or completes the statement. *PRINT THE LETTER OF THE CORRECT ANSWER IN THE SPACE AT THE RIGHT.*

1. On January 1, a family was receiving supplementary monthly public assistance of $280   1.____
    for food, $240 for rent, and $140 for other necessities. In the spring, their rent rose by
    10%, and their rent allotment was adjusted accordingly. In the summer, due to the death
    of a family member, their allotments for food and other necessities were reduced by 1/7.
    Their monthly allowance check in the fall should be

    A. $624   B. $644   C. $664   D. $684

2. Twice a month, a certain family receives a $340 general allowance for rent, food, and   2.____
    clothing expenses. In addition, the family receives a specific supplementary allotment for
    utilities of $384 a year, which is added to their semi-monthly check.
    If the general allowance alone is reduced by 5%, what will be the TOTAL amount of
    their next semi-monthly check?

    A. $323   B. $339   C. $340   D. $355

3. If each supervising clerk in a certain unit sees an average of 9 clients in a 7-hour day and   3.____
    there are 15 supervising clerks in the unit, APPROXIMATELY how many clients will be
    seen in a 35-hour week?

    A. 315   B. 405   C. 675   D. 945

4. In one day, an aide receives 18 inquiries by phone and 27 inquiries in person.   4.____
    What percentage of the inquiries received that day were by phone?

    A. 33%   B. 40%   C. 45%   D. 60%

5. If the weekly paychecks for 5 employees are $258.64, $325.48, $287.34, $271.50, and   5.____
    $313.12, then the combined weekly income for the 5 employees is

    A. $1,455.68   B. $1,456.08   C. $1,461.68   D. $1,474.08

6. Suppose that there are 17 aides working in an office where many community complaints   6.____
    are received by telephone. In one ten-day period, 4,250 calls were received.
    If the same number of calls were received each day, and the aides divided the work
    load equally, about how many calls did each aide respond to daily?

    A. 25   B. 35   C. 75   D. 250

7. Suppose that an assignment was divided among 5 aides. If the first aide spent 67 hours   7.____
    on the assignment, the second aide spent 95 hours, the third aide spent 52 hours, the
    fourth aide spent 78 hours, and the fifth aide spent 103 hours, what was the AVERAGE
    amount of time spent by each aide on the assignment?
    _____ hours.

    A. 71   B. 75   C. 79   D. 83

8. If there are 240 employees in a center and 1/3 are absent on the day of a bad snow-storm, how many employees were at work in the center on that day?

   A. 80   B. 120   C. 160   D. 200

8.____

9. Suppose that an aide takes 25 minutes to prepare a letter to a client.
If the aide is assigned to prepare 9 letters on a certain day, how much time should she set aside for this task? _____ hours.

   A. 3 3/4   B. 4 1/4   C. 4 3/4   D. 5 1/4

9.____

10. Suppose that a certain center uses both Form A and Form B in the course of its daily work and that Form A is used 4 times as often as Form B.
If the total number of both forms used in one week is 750, how many times was Form A used?

   A. 100   B. 200   C. 400   D. 600

10.____

11. Suppose a center has a budget of $2,185.40 from which 8 desks costing $156.10 apiece must be bought.
How many additional desks can be ordered from this budget after the 8 desks have been purchased?

   A. 4   B. 6   C. 9   D. 14

11.____

12. When researching a particular case, a team of 16 aides was asked to check through 234 folders to obtain the necessary information.
If half the aides worked twice as fast as the other half, and the slow group checked through 12 folders each hour, about how long would it take to complete the assignment? _____ hours.

   A. 4 1/4   B. 5   C. 6   D. 6 1/2

12.____

13. The difference in the cost of two typewriters is $56.64. If the less expensive typewriter costs $307.22, what is the cost of the other typewriter?

   A. $343.86   B. $344.06   C. $363.86   D. $364.06

13.____

14. At the start of a year, a family was receiving a public assistance grant of $382 twice a month, on the 1st and 15th of each month. On March 1, their rent allowance was decreased from $150 to $142 a month since they had moved to a smaller apartment. On August 1, their semi-monthly food allowance, which had been $80.40, was raised by 10%. In that year, the TOTAL amount of money disbursed to this family was

   A. $4,544.20   B. $6,581.40   C. $9,088.40   D. $9,168.40

14.____

15. It is discovered that a client has received double public assistance for 2 months by having been enrolled at two service centers of the Department of Social Services.
The client should have received $168 twice a month instead of the double amount. He now agrees to repay the money by equal deductions from his public assistance check over a period of 12 months. What will the amount of his NEXT check be?

   A. $112   B. $140   C. $154   D. $160

15.____

16. Suppose a study is being made of the composition of 3,550 families receiving public assistance. Of the first 1,050 families reviewed, 18% had four or more children.
If, in the remaining number of families, the percentage with four or more children is half as high as the percentage in the group already reviewed, then the percentage of families with four or more children in the entire group of families is MOST NEARLY

    A. 12   B. 14   C. 16   D. 27

16.____

17. Suppose that food prices have risen 13%, and an increase of the same amount has been granted in the food allotment given to people receiving public assistance.
If a family has been receiving $810 a month, 35% of which is allotted for food, then the TOTAL amount of public assistance this family receives per month will be changed to

    A. $805.42   B. $840.06   C. $846.86   D. $899.42

17.____

18. Assume that the food allowance is to be raised 5% in August but will be retroactive for four months to April.
The retroactive allowance is to be divided into equal sections and added to the public assistance checks for August, September, October, November, and December. A family which has been receiving $840 monthly, 40% of which was allotted for food, will receive what size check in August?

    A. $853.44   B. $856.80   C. $861.00   D. $870.24

18.____

19. A blind client, who receives $210 public assistance twice a month, inherits 14 shares of stock worth $180 each.
The client is required to sell the stock and spend his inheritance before receiving more public assistance. Using his public assistance allowance as a guide, how many months are his new assets expected to last?

    A. 6   B. 7   C. 8   D. 12

19.____

20. The Department of Social Services has 16 service centers. These centers may be divided into those which are downtown and those which are uptown. Two of the centers are special service centers and are downtown, while the remainder of the centers are general service centers. There is a total of 7 service centers downtown.
The percentage of the general service centers which are uptown is MOST NEARLY

    A. 56   B. 64   C. 69   D. 79

20.____

21. For six months, a family lived in a 4-room apartment where they paid $380 a month. They made an intrasite move to a 4-room apartment where they paid $85 per room a month for six months.
Comparing the two six-month periods, the TOTAL amount of money the family saved by making the intrasite move was

    A. $240   B. $290   C. $430   D. $590

21.____

22. To calculate a tenant's usable income, you should make Social Security deductions of 4.4 percent on salary up to a maximum of $9,000 and State Disability deductions of .5 percent on salary up to $3,000.
What does a tenant's combined deduction amount to if his annual salary is $13,400?

    A. $411.00   B. $568.60   C. $619.60   D. $700.00

22.____

23. If the temporary relocation expenses for housing are set at $18 per day for one adult and $10 per day for each additional person in a room, how much money is allowed for a woman and four children temporarily relocated in one room for a period of six days?

    A. $168   B. $348   C. $378   D. $518

23.____

24. According to relocation policy, a family relocating to private housing from federally-aided or certain other sites will be granted a relocation payment. This payment equals the difference between 1/5 of the family's yearly income and the scheduled yearly rent for a standard apartment for their size family.
Suppose a 2-person family whose yearly income is $12,900 has been unable to obtain public housing and so finds a one-bedroom private apartment. The scheduled rent for a one-bedroom apartment appropriate for their occupancy is $240 a month. What payment will they receive?

    A. $240   B. $288   C. $300   D. $410

24.____

25. A family on a housing relocation site is paying $410 per month for rent. This represents 25% of their gross monthly income.
If the husband earns 4/5 of their total combined monthly income, how much does the wife earn per month?

    A. $328   B. $540   C. $1,280   D. $1,600

25.____

KEY (CORRECT ANSWERS)

1.	A		11.	B
2.	B		12.	D
3.	C		13.	C
4.	B		14.	D
5.	B		15.	B
6.	A		16.	A
7.	C		17.	C
8.	C		18.	D
9.	A		19.	A
10.	D		20.	B

21.	A
22.	A
23.	B
24.	C
25.	A

SOLUTIONS TO PROBLEMS

1. After spring, the rent allotment should be $(240+24) = $264 After the summer, the reduced allotment for food and other necessities should be $[(280+140)-1/7(280+140)] = $[(420 - 1/7(420)] = $(420-60) = $360. ∴ The monthly check in the fall including rent, food, and other necessities should be $360 + $264 = $624

2. Amount of general allowance in the family's semi-monthly check = $340. Amount of utilities allotment in the family's semi-monthly check: $$\left(\frac{384}{12}\times\frac{1}{2}\right) = \$16$$ Amount of general allowance in family's semi-monthly check after a 5% reduction = $340 less 5% of $340 = $(340-17) = $323 Total amount of the next month's semi-monthly check: Reduced general allowance + utilities allotment = $323 + $16 = $339

3. During 7 hours, a total of (15)(9) = 135 clients can be seen. Thus, in 35 hours, a total of (135)(5) = 675 clients will be seen.

4. 18/(18+27) = .40 = 40%

5. $258.64 + $325.48 + $287.34 + $271.50 + $313.12 = $1456.08

6. 4250 / 10 = 425 calls per day. Then, 425 / 17 = 25

7. (67+95+52+78+103) / 5 = 79 hours

8. Number present = (240)(2/3) = 160

9. (25)(9) = 225 min. = 3 hrs. 45 min. = 3 3/4 hrs.

10. Let x, 1/4x = number of forms A, B, respectively. Then, x + 1/4 x = 750. Solving, x = 600

11. $2185.40 - (8)($156.10) = $936.60. Then, $936.60 v 156.10 = 6 desks

12. Since the slow group did 12 folders each hour, the faster group did 24 folders each hour. Then, 234 / (12+24) = 6 1/2 hrs.

13. Expensive typewriter costs $307.22 + $56.64 = $363.86

14. For months of January and February, the amount the family receives is $(382x2x2) = $1528
For months of March through July, the family receives $(764-8) x 5 = $3780
For months of August through December, the family receives $(756+16.08) x 5 = $3860.40 The total amount of money disbursed to this family is $1528 + $3780 + $3860.40 = $9,168.40

15. The overpayment for 2 months = ($168)(4) = $672. If this is paid back over 12 months, each month's amount is reduced by $672 / 12 = $56. Then, each check (semi-monthly) is reduced by $28. His next check will be $168 - $28 = $140

16. (1050)(.18) + (2500)(.09) = 414. Then, 414 / 3550 = 12%

17. ($810)(.35) = $283.50 originally allotted for food. The new food allotment = ($283.50)(1.13) = $320.355. The total assistance now = $810 - $283.50 + $320.355 = $846.855 or $846.86

18. ($840)(.40) = $336 per month for food. The new food allowance = ($336)(1.05) = $352.80 per month. The difference of $16.80 is retroactive to April, which means ($16.80)(9) = $151.20 additional money for August through December. Each check for these 5 months will be increased by $15.20 / 5 = 30.24. Thus, the check in August = $840 + 30.24 = $870.24

19. ($180)(14) = $2520. Then, $2520 / $420 = 6 months

20. 5 general are -downtown; ... 9 of 14 general are uptown; 9 / 14 $\approx$ 64%.

21. ($85)(4) = $340 per month. Savings per month = $380 - $340 = $40 For six months, the savings = $240

22. ($9000)(.044) + ($3000)(.005) = $411 total deductions

23. ($18+$40)(6) = $348 relocation expenses

24. ($240)(12) - (1/5)($12,900) = $300 relocation payment

25. $410 ÷ .25 = $1640. The wife earns (1640)(1/5) = $328 each month.

———

TEST 2

DIRECTIONS: Each question or incomplete statement is followed by several suggested answers or completions. Select the one that BEST answers the question or completes the statement. *PRINT THE LETTER OF THE CORRECT ANSWER IN THE SPACE AT THE RIGHT.*

1. A project tenant who owns and drives a taxicab for a living, reports for a three-month period, an income of $6,250 after operating expenses of $1,300 have been considered. In addition, his tips are valued at 12% of his income before operating expenses. An estimate of his yearly income is MOST NEARLY   1.____

    A. $22,000   B. $23,000   C. $28,000
    D. $28,500   E. $29,000

2. The maximum annual subsidy which can be paid by the State toward the operation of any low-rent housing project is the sum of the annual interest on the total original loan for building the project and 1% of the portion of the loan actually spent.
    If the original loan for a project was $8,000,000 at 1 3/4% interest, but only $7,500,000 was actually spent, then the MAXIMUM annual subsidy is   2.____

    A. $140,000   B. $145,000   C. $215,000
    D. $220,000   E.   271,250

3. In 2003, the cost of repairs and maintenance at a certain housing project was $5,589 more than in 2002, representing an increase of 4.6%. A further increase at the same rate was anticipated for 2004.
    The cost of repairs and maintenance in 2004 was MOST NEARLY   3.____

    A. $127,100
    B. $132,700
    C. $132,900
    D. $133,000
    E.   an amount which cannot be determined from the given data

4. Each day a delivery truck used by the Housing Authority travels 25 miles from a project to a storehouse and 25 miles on the return trip. It travels at the rate of 30 miles per hour going to the storehouse and at the rate of 20 miles per hour returning.
    The average rate, in miles per hour, for the roundtrip is MOST NEARLY   4.____

    A.   24
    B.   25
    C.   26
    D.   the square root of 600
    E.   an amount which cannot be determined from the given data 0

5. A report on the first 6,000 applications for apartments in a certain project containing 1,400 apartments indicated that those who were ineligible fell into four categories: 2,800 ineligible for reason A, 600 ineligible for reason B, 1,200 ineligible for reason C, and 400 ineligible for reason D.
    If the same proportions continue for the remaining 21,500 applications, then the percentage of eligible applicants who can be given apartments in the project is MOST NEARLY   5.____

    A.   25   B.   30   C.   33   D.   40   E.   60

6. The number of applications for apartments in low-rent housing projects was 40,000 in 1999. The number of applications increased 5% in 2000, and increased again in 2001 by 6% over the 2000 total.
   The percentage by which the 2001 figures exceed the 1999 figures is

   A.   5.3   B.   6.0   C.   11.0   D.   11.3   E.   30.0

   6.____

7. A rectangular lot, 75 feet by 11.0 feet, was purchased as part of a project site for $28,500.
   The price per square foot of this lot is MOST NEARLY

   A. $2.85   B. $3.45   C. $3.95   D. $30.00   E. $30.95

   7.____

8. It has been estimated that 125 kilowatt-hours of electricity are used each month in one average Housing Authority apartment at a cost of 14.8 cents per kilowatt-hour.
   On this basis, the total cost of the electricity used in one year in a project containing 1,400 apartments is MOST NEARLY

   A. $20,000   B. $25,000   C. $200,000
   D. $250,000   E. $2,000,000

   8.____

9. The walls and ceilings of 20 rooms are to be painted with the same kind of paint, each room being 15 feet long, 12 feet wide, and 10 feet high. Each room contains two windows, each 3 feet by 6 feet, and a door 3 feet by 8 feet, which are not to be painted. One gallon of paint covers 400 square feet of surface.
   The number of gallons of paint needed is MOST NEARLY

   A.   33   B.   34   C.   35   D.   36   E.   75

   9.____

10. A group of buildings is valued at $11,500,000. Assume that the cost of fire insurance for these buildings is 5.3 cents per $100 of valuation per year.
    The cost of fire insurance for one year is MOST NEARLY

    A. $600   B. $6,000   C. $20,000
    D. $60,000   E. $2,000,000

    10.____

11. Of the 15 employees in a certain unit, one-third earn $27,600 per year, three earn $32,600, one earns $46,400, and the rest earn $33,800.
    The average salary of the employees of this unit is MOST NEARLY

    A. $31,000   B. $32,000   C. $33,000   D. $34,000   E. $35,000

    11.____

12. Four pieces, each 2'5 3/8" long, are cut from a piece of pipe 16 1/2' long.
    The length of the remaining piece of pipe is

    A.   6'8 1/2"   B.   6'10"   C.   6'10 3/8"
    D.   6'11 1/8"   E.   9'9 1/2"

    12.____

13. A tenant earns E dollars a month, spends S dollars a week, and saves the rest.
    The tenant's yearly savings can be expressed by

    A.   12(E-4S)   B.   12E - 52S   C.   12(E-S)
    D.   52(E-4S)   E.   E - S

    13.____

14. A unit of fifteen Housing Assistants has been assigned the job of interviewing applicants. Each interview takes 35 minutes, and an additional 10 minutes is needed for making entries and notes. The last interview each day is always scheduled so that it can be completed that day.
The number of applicants who can be interviewed in a week, consisting of five 7-hour days, is MOST NEARLY

    A. 375   B. 525   C. 675   D. 700   E. 725   14.____

15. A review of the 14,000 applications for apartments in a certain project containing 1,200 apartments indicated that 4,800 applicants were eligible and 6,400 were ineligible. No decision could be reached on the remaining applications because certain necessary information was omitted by the applicants, but it was assumed that the proportion of eligible and ineligible applicants would remain the same as in those already decided.
On the basis of these figures, the percentage of eligible applicants who can be given apartments in the project is   15.____

    A. under 17%   B. 17%   C. 20%
    D. 25%   E. 33 1/3%

16. An oil burner in a housing development burns 76 gallons of fuel oil per hour. At 9 A.M. on a very cold day, the superintendent asks the Housing Manager to put in an emergency order for more fuel oil. At that time, he reports that he has on hand 266 gallons. At noon, he again comes to the manager, notifying him that no oil has been delivered.
The MAXIMUM amount of time that he can continue to furnish heat without receiving more oil is   16.____

    A. no more time   B. 1/2 hour   C. 1 hour
    D. 1 1/2 hours   E. 2 hours

17. As a result of reports received by the Housing Authority concerning the reputed ineligibility of 756 tenants because of above-standard incomes, an intensive check of their employers has been ordered. Four housing assistants have been assigned to this task. At the end of 6 days at 7 hours each, they have checked on 336 tenants. In order to speed up the investigation, two more housing assistants are assigned to this point.
If they worked at the same rate, the number of additional 7-hour days it would take to complete the job is MOST NEARLY   17.____

    A. 1   B. 3   C. 5   D. 7   E. 9

18. A municipal aide on a special trip is returning to his office from a point 17 1/2 miles away, and makes the return trip to his office at an average speed of 25 miles an hour, except for a 15-minute stopover at one point to get a flat tire fixed.
The time it should take him to reach his office is MOST NEARLY _____ minutes.   18.____

    A. 12   B. 22   C. 36   D. 42   E. 57

19. A district office has an assigned staff of 320 employees. Of this number, 25% are not available for duty due to illness, vacations, and other reasons. Of those who are available for duty, 1/8 are assigned to auditing and special projects, and the rest to handling the workload. The ACTUAL number of employees available for handling the workload is   19.____

    A. 350   B. 310   C. 270   D. 210   E. 180

20. Two dozen shuttlecocks and four badminton rackets are to be purchased for a play-   20.____
    ground. The shuttlecocks are priced at $3.60 each, and the rackets at $27.50 each. The
    playground receives a discount of 30% from these prices. The TOTAL cost of this equip-
    ment is

    A. $72.90   B. $114.30   C. $13.7.48   D. $186.00   E. $220.70

21. On January 1, a family was receiving a public assistance allowance of $185 for food, $53   21.____
    for clothing, $17.50 for utilities, and $22 for personal needs, all semi-monthly, and a
    monthly allowance of $550 for rent. On May 1, the rent allowance was increased by 12%
    but all other allowances remained the same for the rest of the year.
    The TOTAL amount of money granted this family during the year was

    A. $10,528   B. $13,262   C. $13,788
    D. $21,056   E. $27,676

22. It has been decided to make changes in food allotments to clients receiving public assis-   22.____
    tance to conform to changes in food costs. Of the food allowance, 30% is intended for
    meat, 30% for fruits and vegetables, 25% for groceries, and 15% for dairy products.
    Assume that meat prices have gone up 10%, fruit and vegetable prices have gone down
    20%, grocery prices have gone up 5%, and dairy prices have remained the same.
    For a family that has been receiving $400 per month for food, the new monthly food
    allowance will be

    A. $333   B. $375   C. $393   D. $403.50   E. $420

23. On January 1, a family was receiving a public assistance allowance of $195 for food, $63   23.____
    for clothing, $27.50 for utilities, and $32 for personal needs, all semi-monthly, and a
    monthly allowance of $510 for rent. On June 1, the rent allowance was increased by
    12%, but all other allowances remained the same for the rest of the year.
    The TOTAL amount of money granted this family during the year was

    A. $13,843.40   B. $14,107.20   C. $14,168.40
    D. $14,474.40   E. $16,886.80

24. A member of a family receiving public assistance amounting to $600 monthly has   24.____
    obtained a part-time job, for which he is paid $40 a day. He is employed 3 days a week.
    His carfare costs $3.00 per day and his lunches $2.00 per day. Assume that there are 4
    1/3 weeks per month. The Department of Welfare requires that net earnings be deducted
    from relief allowances.
    The family's semi-monthly public assistance allowance should be reduced to

    A. $40.00   B. $72.50   C. $96.25   D. $123.75   E. $145.00

25. A couple living in a furnished room has been receiving a public assistance grant of $375   25.____
    semi-monthly and has been paying a weekly rent of $75. The landlord has been granted
    a 12% increase in rent. Assume that a month consists of 4 1/3 weeks.
    The amount of the new semi-monthly grant, including this rent increase, that the cou-
    ple will receive will be MOST NEARLY

    A. $394.50   B. $397   C. $409   D. $514   E. $557

KEY (CORRECT ANSWERS)

1.	D	11.	B
1.	C	12.	A
2.	C	13.	B
3.	A	14.	C
4.	B	15.	C
5.			
6.	D	16.	B
7.	B	17.	C
8.	D	18.	E
9.	A	19.	D
10.	B	20.	C
		21.	C
		22.	C
		23.	C
		24.	B
		25.	A

SOLUTIONS TO PROBLEMS

1. For 3 months, income = $6250 + (.12)($7550) = $7156 Then, annual income = ($7154)(4) = $28,624, closest to $28,500

2. Maximum annual subsidy = ($8,000,000)(.0175) + (.01)($7,500,000) = $215,000

3. Cost in 2002 = $5589 / .046 = $121,500. The cost in 2003 = $121,500 + $5589 = $127,089. This means the cost in 2004 = ($127,089)(1.046) = $132,900

4. Average rate = total distance / total time = (25+25) ÷ (25/30 + 25/20) = 24 mph.

5. Out of 6000, number of eligible = 6000 - 2800 - 600 - 1200 - 400 = 1000. Thus, for 27,500 applications, (1/6)(27,500) = 4583 would be eligible. Finally, 1400 ÷ 4583 ≈ 30%

6. Number of applications in 2000 = (40,000)(1.05) = 42,000 Number of applications in 2001 = (42,000)(1.06) = 44,520 Then, (44,520-40,000) ÷ 40,000 = 11.3%

7. $28,500 ÷ [(75X110)] = $3.45 per sq.ft.

8. Total cost = (125)(.148)(12)(1400) = $310,800; closest to choice D of $250,000

9. Painted area of each room = (2)(15)(10) + (2)(12)(10) + (15)(12) - (2)(3)(6) - (3)(8) = 660 sq.ft. So, (20)(660) = 13,200 sq.ft. to be painted in all rooms. Finally, 13,200 / 400 = 33 gallons of paint needed

10. Insurance cost = (.053)($11,500,000)/$100 = $6095, closest to $6000

11. [(5)($27,600)+(3)($32,600)+(1)(46,400)+(6)($33,800)]/15 = $32,333, closest to $32,000

12. 16 1/2 - (4)(2'5 3/8") = 16'6" - 8'21 1/2" = 16'6" - 9'9 1/2" = 6'8 1/2"

13. Annual savings = 12E - 52S

14. $7 \div \dfrac{3}{4} = 9.\overline{3}$, which means each interviewer can interview a maximum of 9 applicants each day. Then, (5)(9)(15) = 675 applicants.

15. 4800/(4800+6400) = 3/7 eligible. On that assumption, there would be (3/7)(14,000) = 6000 eligible applicants. Then, 1200/6000 = 20%

16. 266 - (3)(76) = 38 gallons of oil left. Then, 38 / 76 =1/2 hour

17. (6)(7)(4) = 168 hrs. to check on 336 tenants. This means 2 tenants require 1 man-hour. Now, (6)(7)(x days) = man-hrs. would be needed to check the remaining 420 tenants. This requires 210 man-hours. So, (6)(7)(x) = 210. Solving, x = 5

18. $\dfrac{17.5}{25}$ = .7 hr. = 42 min. Total time = 42 + 15 = 57 min.

19. Number available = 320[1-.25-(1/8)(.75)] = 210

20. Total cost = (.70)[(24)($3.60)+(4)(27.50)] = $137.48

21. From January through April, amount = (8)($185+$53+$17,50+$22) + (4)($550) = $4420.
From May through December, amount = (16)($185+$53+$17.50+$22) + (8)($550)(1.12)
= $9368 Total annual amount = $4420 + $9368 = $13,788

22. Meat allowance = ($400)(.30)(1.10) = $132; fruit and vegetable allowance =
($400)(.30)(.80) = $96; grocery allowance = ($400)(.25)(1.05) = $105; dairy allowance =
($400)(,15) = $60 New monthly allowance = $132 + $96 + $105 + $.60 = $393

23. From January through May, amount = (10)($195+$63+$27.50+$32) + (5)($510) = $5725.
From June through December, amount = (14)($195+$63+$27.50+$32) + (7)($510)(1.12)
= $8443.40. Total annual amount = $5725 + $8443.40 = $14,168.40

24. Monthly assistance should be reduced to $600 - [(40)(3)(4 1/3) - ($5)(3)(4 1/3)] = $145.
So, the semi-monthly amount is now $145 / 2 = $72.50

25. ($75) (4 1/3) / 2 = $162.50 = original semi-monthly rent.
New semi-monthly rent = (162.50)(1.12) = $182. Since this represents an increase of
$19.50, the new semi-monthly grant will be increased to $375 + $19.50 = $394.50

HUMAN RELATIONS

TABLE OF CONTENTS

HUMAN RELATIONS

Introduction

The success of any enterprise is largely determined by its people: Their individual competences, the values they hold, and the quality of their leadership. This generalization stresses attributes important in business, industry, government, or institutional operations, the lack of which produces, at the least, inefficiency and, at the worst, disruption or even destruction of enterprises.

Disaster and civil defense emergency conditions complicate the effective use of personnel, the attainment of objectives, and the control of the citizenry in the affected areas. Normal interpersonal and intergroup relations tend to deteriorate and individual, group and community effectiveness is lost.

Most of us recognize that understanding and practicing good human relations is important under normal circumstances, but under ordinary conditions most interpersonal adjustments are made simply, easily, and often unconsciously. They are habituated responses learned, practiced, and found effective during countless repetitions of personal contacts. Effective human relations under emergency conditions, however, may be more difficult and their attainment becomes a serious matter for study and understanding.

The phrase "human relations" includes subject matter almost as broad as the study of mankind itself. Many books have been written on the subject. In this brief chapter we can deal only summarily with a few of the more important concepts involved in relations among human beings.

Facts About People

It is a truism that people are alike in some ways but different in other ways. Handling human relations situations wisely requires sensitivity to individual differences. Physically some people are short and some tall, some fat and some thin. Some adhere to one religion, some to another, and some to none. One person may never have gone to school while his neighbor may have had six years or more of college. Yet the former may be wealthy land the latter relatively poor. One may be an outcast in his neighborhood, one well liked, and still another socially prominent. The first may be a gentle recluse and the last aggressive and domineering. More than likely each of us in large measure reflects the attitudes of our parents or, if we have grown away from these, of a group of our peers. There can be no doubt that wej are products of both our heredity and our environment. The interrelationship of various facets of both determine what we are physically, intellectually, and emotionally.

We must recognize that each of us is an individual. Each has his own physique, level of intelligence, special skills and problems, and his own set of beliefs, and prejudice. The latter may include either fear or contempt of the law. Knowing people and recognizing their differences, their strong points and weaknesses, will make us more effective as we attempt to handle emergency conditions and to achieve a measure of normalcy.

While no simple set of "how to" rules can be formulated which will fit all, or even most, human relations situations, a good general principle to keep in mind is the Golden Rule: "Do unto others as you would that they should do unto you"--to which we might add the corollary: *if you had their individual differences.* Therefore, to apply this principle you will need to study people, and especially their *differences* to be able to "put yourself in the other person's place."

Facts About Race

The term race has many meanings to many people. To some it simply means a group of people descended from a common ancestry and consisting of persons who have similar *physical characteristics*. It is in this sense that many speak of whites, Indians, or black. Others tend tc think of races in terms of *nationalities*, such as Italians, Greeks, or Norwegians, insofar as these names denote people coming from various countries or cultures. When majority and minority groups live side by side, a person who essentially is similar to those of the majority, but who has a trace of the minority group characteristics frequently is grouped with the latter. Even competent anthropoligists are not in agreement about what constitutes a race and what distinguishes one race from another, Mingling of human stock has gone on throughout recorded history and relative distinctions based on so-called racial characteristics (such as color of skin, hair, etc.) continue to become more obscure.

It is significant that no basic psychological differences between so-called races have been scientifically established. Superficial differences do exist, tend to become exaggerated, and produce commonly accepted stereotypes. It can, in fact, be reasonably concluded that greater psychological differences exist among people of each race than exist among races.

Superiority of one race over another, long an emotional crutch for the personally inadequate and a rallying cry to international and economic conflict, simply cannot be demonstrated. Like it or not, depending on our personal convictions, it can honestly be said that we are "brothers under the skin."

To be very specific, the "knowledge" we commonly hold about race is really an expression of attitudes that we have come to accept and a product of what we have learned to believe.

Relearning some of one's early conditioning about race, or learning to minimize it or compensate for it, is necessary for many people if they are to function effectively in situations involving relations with people of other "races."

Responsibility of Government

For government to serve its purpose fully it must not only apply the law equally and without favoritism, but it must also provide equal protection and service to all. This position can be accepted as an essential principle of the American creed. Nonetheless, diligent effort must always be applied to make this principle a fact of life to all of our people. Therefore, the law itself must be the rule by which we live and work. There can be no fact of a citizen's makeup-color, religion, or economic or social status-that will change his relative position under the law. Poor man, beggar, merchant or thief, although they may conduct themselves differently and hold different beliefs, are each entitled to a common application of the law. It thus becomes imperative that while on duty the individual officer submerge any of his prejudices and beliefs which are contrary to the law and contrary to the above principle. The most critical factor in producing such professional, objective law enforcement action is that he not bend the law to enforce his own code of conduct or utilize his authority out of spite against those who have antagonized him personally.

The police agency's protection and service must be allocated equally and applied freely to all. The agency serves all of the people and neither the status of an individual citizen nor an officer's attitude toward him should influence the agency's kind or level of service.

This composite result of all our interpersonal and interagency contacts is essentially based on job performance and the competence of the agency and of each employee. This refers not only to specific goals which are attained but also to the method by which they are attained and the conduct of all participating employees. An image of an agency gained through a formal public relations program can at best be of only superficial value if it does not reflect the actual worth of the agency. This, in essence, is the distinction between reputations and character. Reputation based on sound characters has lasting value; reputation other-wise based is transient and of dubious value.

There must be a thorough knowledge of human relations by personnel of all ranks. The practice of sound and understanding human relations is bound to strengthen and deepen the department's public relations and to give it lasting character.

Subordination of the officer's personal biases, prejudices, and beliefs to the policy of the department is essential in the handling of incidents and people. If an officer believes his own position is right, but is contrary to that of the agency, he may properly attempt to persuade his superiors to his point of view. He must recognize, however, that so long as the agency policy continues, he must conform to it meticulously.

It is simpler to prescribe and require conformity to regulations and procedures which influence public relations than it is to change a man's basic beliefs. If agency policy is based on human understanding, common sense requires that it not only be understood, but also accepted: hence the importance of personnel training in both human relations and public relations.

Human Relations Under Stress

Although human relations to the stress of emergency conditions will vary, they will tend to follow the pattern which is normal to each individual. Individual adjustment to cir-cumstances is usually rapid and effective. Within his own limitations and capabilities each individual will attempt to "cany on." Most will respond to effective leadership and under such leadership may be expected to perform reasonably well under whatever cir-cumstances arise.

However, if one person "panics" or loses control of himself while in the company of others there is a tendency for his behavior to communicate itself to those about him. There is, therefore, an immediate need to identify any one who shows signs of such behavior. Two courses are then open. First,

the person may simply be isolated. This will avoid the contagious effect. Second, he may be given treatment that may involve the use of sedatives on a doctor's orders; other med-ical measures; use of a psychiatrist, if cir-cumstances permit; supportive efforts of lay persons who can assist the disturbed person to reorient himself. For example, this may sometimes be accomplished by giving him work to do which occupies his mind and reduces his apprehensions. The person who emotionally seeks a scapegoat may also be a source of serious problems. If he is of a dominating nature he may quickly rally to his "cause" many others who are seeking emo-tional release, a sense of self-importance, and group identification. Such measures as isolation and treatment may be necessary to minimize his harmful influence.

It is to be expected that there wfll be some unusual human reactions in time of civil defense emergency or other major disaster that can be considered quite nor-mal. We may expect that these would be manifested in forms less serious than those which we have been discussing. For exam-ple, there may be increased muscular ten-sion and bodily responses, and some accompanying psychological manifestations such as excitement and confusion. It is to be stressed, however, that such conditions as a certain stiffness of movement, heavy perspi-ration, rapid breathing, sudden talkative-ness, or unusual quiet are all normal reactions to, unusual conditions.

Disaster reactions become abnormal and can be classified as disaster fatigue only when the kinds of conditions indicated above do not pass away quickly and sponta-neously without treatment. If a person does not lose or quickly regains his effectiveness his reaction may be considered normal.

Mild disaster fatigue normally will soon pass without treatment and with no ill effects. It is not usually a concern to emer-gency personnel except as it somewhat reduces a person's effectiveness. However, if it does not disappear or becomes slightly more severe we may classify it as moderate disaster fatigue. If the fatigue does nut pass or if it tends to become progressively more severe, treatment is indicated and persons so affected should have medical attention. In the case of severe fatigue, medical attention is mandatory. Unless medical service is promptly available the person may be past susceptibility to treatment and quick recovery. Immediate medical treatment may return persons to normal, prevent increased fatigue and loss of effectiveness, and avoid unusual problems of prolonged care and treatment.

Behavior in Disaster

Concern of civil authorities with people extends, in time, from the normal conditions before disaster to the relatively stable conditions finally achieved after the disaster, whether or not they, in fact, resemble the normal predisaster conditions. It is important to remember that it is during the predisaster normal conditions people must be prepared for disaster. This includes preparing individuals to anticipate disaster conditions, and to accept group organization and training to minimize its effects.

If adequate indoctrination and training have been provided, the warning phase should pose no special problems, but should be a period in which official disaster plans can be placed in effect with individuals taking predetermined precautions, or proceeding to designated posts. Emergency personnel should be on the alert for signs of panic or other disturbances, and be prepared to take appropriate actions.

The impact phase is a critical one because of its disruption of the community and its normal activities. Power may be lost, transportation may break down, and entire geographic areas may be physically isolated or destroyed. This period will be a serious test of plans, organization, uncertainty and confusion. Persons will have disaster fatigue in all of its manifestations and degrees. Big problems will demand attention and action. As the postimpact phase is entered, recovering from the effects of the disaster will

move toward the resumption of normalcy. At this point special attention must be given to problems of disaster fatigue, prompt treatment provided for those in need, and accommodations provided for those who may require extended care. Many who survive the critical emergency period may now have delayed emotional reactions, and attention must' be given to identifying these people and providing them with necessary case.

Effects of Disruption of Living Habits

Living in a shelter or relocation area will be an experience with which the average person can draw no comparison from his experience. Unless he has been in military service, or in prison, it will probably be his first experience as an adult in living closely with others not of his own choice. Under these circumstances he can not simply "be himself." There must be provided effective patterns of group living and he must learn to adjust to them. He will remain an individual, but he must accept a unique responsibility for self-subordination to group goals and conduct. It must be recognized that this, for many, will be difficult, and it must be given due weight by leaders and their staff to induce harmonious, cooperative, and productive patterns of group living.

A special problem will be the presence of many persons separated from members of their families. Sometimes this will be the heartbreaking and final separation of death, and at other times the perhaps even more emotion-laden situation of uncertainty about loved ones. Every effort must be made to keep together, or to reunite, members of families.

Other problems will be created by the presence, in some cases, of criminals, drug addicts, and other deviates. The exigencies of group living may well result in magnification of problems of "normal" people which are more manageable in normal living. For example, tobacco smokers will need to be controlled for the welfare of all of the inhabitants of a shelter. Habitual smokers deprived of their regular gratification, whether because of shelter rules or because their supply of tobacco is exhausted, will experience discomfort or hardship, and may be irritable. Sexual advances may take place which would not be likely in the same group of people if they were gathered together under more normal circumstances.

Most persons, in establishing their own patterns of living, seek harmonious relationships. This often means that people group themselves in communities where there are common backgrounds of race, nationality, religion, education, and employment. Living under emergency conditions, will seldom allow this. People who do not know or "understand" each other will find themselves living closely together under conditions of privation and hardship. In such circumstances, adjustment may be difficult.

In an emergency there is enforced restriction or mobility. People cannot get away from others whom they would not normally choose as companions. Again, for this reason, everyone must accept unusual responsibilities for harmonious and cooperative living, and leaders must make every effort to minimize frictions imposed by the lack of mobility.

For all practical purposes, normal pursuits will not be available to more than a few. Leaders must seek out opportunities to keep people productively occupied both as individuals and as groups.

The above considerations suggest that leaders and their staff, including law enforcement personnel, will need to *be* capable of diagnosing and managing human relations situations within the group. Fortu-

nately, research in human behavior provides much in the way of guidelines for such an endeavor, and Federal DCPA courses afford opportunities for leaders and their staffs to increase their capabilities in such matters.

In spite of all of the problems, leaders must keep living conditions as bearable as possible. Since no single way of living wfll be normal for anyone, the problems of personal adjustment and group leadership will be difficult. Accordingly, leaders win have to be on the alert constantly to anticipate difficulties of interpersonal and intergroup relations in time to take preventive action. Avoidance of group tensions and conflict is by far the better course of action than attempts to correct or overcome problem situations once they have developed.

It is a first responsibility of leadership to give confidence to those in the group. While this confidence may sometimes result from an outstanding "natural leader," it is more often the result of a studied effort to build it. The people must be kept as well informed as possible about what is going on in the disaster area.

Leaders must organize and direct activities which may be productive or divertive in nature, but must be meaningful to those who participate. Leaders must be honest about problems, positive in then- actions, and impartial and humane in carrying out their decisions. The kind of leadership exerted wfll largely determine community morale and smoothness of the transition back to more nearly normal living.

9 781731 801289